Classic
Comparative
Anthropology

Classic Comparative Anthropology

Studies from the Tradition

Philip Carl Salzman

McGill University

WAVELAND

PRESS, INC.

Long Grove, Illinois

For information about this book, contact:
Waveland Press, Inc.
4180 IL Route 83, Suite 101
Long Grove, IL 60047-9580
(847) 634-0081
info@waveland.com
www.waveland.com

10-digit ISBN 1-57766-710-7
13-digit ISBN 978-1-57766-710-0

Printed in the United States of America

7 6 5 4 3 2 1

Contents

Preface

In my senior undergraduate seminar on "Comparative Anthropology" at McGill University in Montreal, students read original examples of classic comparative analysis. In our three-month-long semester, the students are assigned 11 articles and two books that illustrate the various ways that social and cultural anthropologists have used comparison to advance their understanding of human lives. Reading the original works is recommended, but time-consuming.

This small book is for readers who would like an introduction to classic comparative anthropology, but who cannot devote months to reading complete original works. The objective of the book is to offer brief accounts of classic comparative anthropology, including many well-known examples by renown anthropologists, as well as a few recent examples in the classic spirit. Of particular interest are the different ways in which classic authors use comparative analysis.

There are some things that this book does not do: It is not comprehensive; it does not attempt to name every author who has used comparative analysis, or mention every study that relies on comparison. It does not recount theoretical and methodological debates about comparative anthropology. Nor does it discuss some recent work that is not in accord with the goals and methods of classic comparative anthropology.

I offer the studies described in this book because I find them informative and illuminating. They are good illustrations of how classic comparison added to knowledge and understanding. For me, they are examples of good anthropology. Please note, however, that any particular account reported here is not necessarily the last word on the subject discussed. Research and debate have continued on some of these subjects, and current views might differ from the conclusions of the study reported.

In their books, professors often thank their students for what they learned from them. This is a nice gesture, but usually highly exaggerated. However, I can truly say that, in my seminar on comparative anthropology, I have learned a lot from my students, almost all of whom were very sweet, and many of whom were extremely bright. I read many good and many truly lovely essays from my students in the seminar. For this reason, I dedicate this book to them.

I also wish to acknowledge Penelope Bertrand, whose Honours Thesis on Cuba I supervised. I have drawn heavily on her work, as indicated in the citations.

Chapter One

Introduction

Comparative analysis is the main method used by social and cultural anthropologists to discover and formulate general knowledge. It is the second stage in anthropological exploration.

The first stage in anthropological research is the ethnographic study of particular societies and cultures. This is usually carried out through field research using the general strategy of "participant observation," which involves living with the people being studied for a considerable time, commonly a year or more, conversing with them, observing them, and trying to understand their world from their point of view. For example, to mention two founders of modern British social anthropology, A. R. Radcliffe-Brown went to the Andaman Islands, off the tip of India, to learn about life there. Bronislaw Malinowski, interned as a foreign national during World War I, famously lived for the better part of five years in the Trobriand Islands of Melanesia. This is how Malinowski (1984[1922]:7–8) describes ethnographic field research:

> Soon after I had established myself in Omarakana (Trobriand Islands), I began to take part, in a way, in the village life, to look forward to the important or festive events, to take personal interest in the gossip and the developments of the small village occurrences; to wake up every morning to a day, presenting itself to me more or less as it does to a native. I would get out from under my mosquito net, to find around me the village life beginning to stir, or the people well advanced in their working day according to the hour and also to the season, for they get up and begin their labours early or late, as work presses. As I went on my morning walk through the village, I could see intimate details of family life, of toilet, cooking, taking of meals; I could see the arrangements for the day's work, people starting on their errands, or groups of men and women busy at some manufacturing tasks. Quarrels, jokes, family scenes, events

1

usually trivial, sometimes dramatic but always significant, formed
the atmosphere of my daily life, as well as of theirs. . . .

Later on in the day, whatever happened was within easy reach, and
there was no possibility of its escaping my notice. Alarms about the
sorcerer's approach in the evening, one or two big, really important
quarrels and rifts within the community, cases of illness, attempted cures and deaths, magical rites which had to be performed, all
these I had not to pursue, fearful of missing them, but they took
place under my very eyes, at my own doorstep, so to speak.

This description would not be far from what most field ethnographers
doing research have experienced since it was published. "Participant
observation" remains the foundational strategy of contemporary ethnographic research.

The results of ethnographic research are particularistic descriptions of unique cultures and societies. The ethnographer has done his
or her job when she or he can provide a detailed report on the place
studied. R-B's ethnographic contribution was *The Andaman Islanders*
(1964[1922]), and Malinowski's unprecedented ouvre included *Argonauts of the Western Pacific* (1984[1922]), *The Sexual Life of the Savages* (1987[1929]), and *Coral Gardens and Their Magic* (1978[1935]).
These ethnographic reports, or "ethnographies," are fascinating works
and are the building blocks of the foundation of anthropology. And yet,
at the same time, we recognize their limitations: they are inherently
knowledge of particular societies and cultures. Yes, we can say, "In the
Andamans, people do X," and "In the Trobriands, people do Y." But how
do we move from the particularistic knowledge of the Andamans and
the Trobriands to more general knowledge about society and culture, or
types of society and culture?

R-B, an early advocate of comparative analysis, in "The Comparative Method in Social Anthropology" (1958:127) says:

The comparative method is therefore one by which we pass from the
particular to the general, from the general to the more general,
with the end in view that we may in this way arrive at the universal, at characteristics which can be found in different forms in all
human societies.

R-B (1958:110) begins with a typically obscure ethnographic example: the division of an Aboriginal tribe in Australia into two groups, one
represented by the eaglehawk and the other by the crow, with membership determined by descent through the female line, and the require-
ment that people must marry into the division to which they do not
belong. (The "technical" terms for this form of organization is "totemi-
cally represented exogamous matrilineal moieties"!) There is a very
similar arrangement among the Haida of the Northwest Coast of North
America, with the eagle and the raven representing the two moieties.

Throughout Australia, there are tribes with moieties, although represented by different birds or other animals. Whichever animals are involved, "the resemblances and differences of animal species are translated," explains R-B (1958:116), "into terms of friendship and conflict, solidarity and opposition. In other words the world of animal life is represented in terms of social relations similar to those of human society."

R-B (1958:118, 124) points out that division into two halves, or moieties, is widespread throughout the world—in Australia, Melanesia, America, and elsewhere, and in the Yin-Yang philosophy of Ancient China—and is significant not only in its institutionalized opposition but also in the corresponding "union of opposites" (Radcliffe-Brown 1958:123). "The relation of the two divisions, which here has been spoken of by the term 'opposition' is one which separates and also unites, and which therefore gives us a rather special kind of social integration." Thus R-B (1958:127) strives "to understand a particular feature of a particular society by first seeing it as a particular instance of a general kind or class of social phenomena, and then by relating it to a certain general, or preferably a universal, tendency in human societies."

R-B (1958:passim) makes a point of distinguishing between, on the one hand, historical analysis, which examines the antecedents of specific cases in order to understand how they developed, and, on the other hand, comparative, sociological analysis, which juxtaposes similar cases with distinct historical origins, to understand the significance of the particular forms of organization and meaning. For example, an historical analysis of the Australian tribe would explore when and how it was decided that there should be two exogamous groups that would intermarry, who decided that relations between the groups would be regulated by "joking relationships," and how and why eaglehawk and crow were chosen as symbols. If such historical information could be found (unlikely in this case), it would illuminate the particularities of this specific case. For a general understanding of this tribe, comparative analysis juxtaposes it with other peoples elsewhere, to show the commonalities and their consequences. In sum, R-B argues that placing a specific case among others through comparative analysis illuminates the sociological significance of a social form found in a particular place by showing its similarity to those of other places, and by so doing forming general knowledge about that social pattern.

A somewhat different approach to comparative analysis is taken by S. F. Nadel in *The Foundation of Social Anthropology* (1953). He (1953:222) sees comparison as the social science equivalent to the experiment in the natural sciences: "We study variations, found and looked for in the data of observation, and correlate them so that from them general regularities emerge. This equivalent of the experiment in the study of society is usually called . . . the comparative method."

Nadel (1953:235–236) illustrates comparative analysis with a study of certain family relations. Among Nuba communities of the Sudan that Nadel studied, in most cases the father had a formal, distant relationship with his children, but in one case the relationship between the father and his children was informal and friendly. At the same time, in most cases the relationship between the grandfather and grandchildren was relaxed and friendly; but in one case the relationship was distant and formal. What was the difference? In most communities, the household was an elementary family of parents and children separate from the household of the grandparents. It was the father who was in charge of discipline. In the one exceptional community, the households were based on extended families, including the grandparents, parents, and children, and the grandfather had disciplinary authority over the household. So we see that disciplinary authority goes with a strict and formal relationship between generations, while the lack of disciplinary authority goes with relaxed and friendly relations. Where the father is the authority figure, his relations with his children are strict, while the relations of the grandfather to his grandchildren are relaxed; where the grandfather is the authority, his relations with his grandchildren are strict, while the relations of the father with his children are relaxed. This suggests a generalization: disciplinary authority and distant, formal relationships go together, while lack of disciplinary authority and relaxed, friendly relations go together. We can have confidence that this general knowledge, based on comparison, is reliable.

Wait a minute, says Nadel (1953:236); not so fast. Other factors can influence family relations and even override the authority/strictness correlation. In West Africa, among the Nupe and Gwari with whom Nadel worked, there were extended families with grandparents in authority, but warm and informal relations between grandfathers and grandsons. How could this be? The grandson is thought to be the reincarnation of a deceased grandfather, and thus the equal to his living grandfather. As equals the grandfather and grandson have a relaxed, friendly, "joking" relationship. So we see, or are shown by Nadel, that even apparently tidy relationships between factors can be disrupted by other influences, in this case spiritual or mystical beliefs. Comparison provided the basis for the generalization about authority and family relations and, at the same time, the additional factor, spiritual beliefs, which complicates the picture.

Nadel (1953:222) argues that as we compare different communities, societies, and cultures, we should see "concomitant variations." How do we find these? By

the analysis of social situations which are at first sight already comparable, that is, which appear to share certain features (modes of action, relationships) while differing in others, or to share their common features with some degree of difference. This first-sight impression will be rendered more precise by demonstrating the extent to which uniformities or differences in any one feature are accompanied by, or "correlated" with, uniformities or differences in others. Hence we are able, finally to isolate the invariant relations between facts upon which all scientific explanations must rest. The concomitant variations (or covariations for short) thus lead us to some such formulas as: If A, then B, for in situations S1, S2, S3. . . . There are A and B; and in situations S4, S5, S6 . . . there are A-changed and B-changed.

In other words, if two factors—such as authority and the nature of relations—vary together, they are likely related to one another (or else to another factor related to both). Once we have identified a possible relation between factors, we can explore the relation further by examining other cases. If the relationship holds over a number of test comparisons, we have a general formulation with some substantiation behind it. This, suggest the advocates of comparative analysis, is an important step to general knowledge.

TYPES OF COMPARATIVE ANALYSES

R-B in the above-mentioned paper emphasizes comparisons that show particular institutions in specific societies as examples of widespread or even universal social arrangements. In contrast, Nadel recommends comparisons as a way of identifying invariant relations between facts—social relations, customs, and beliefs—with the resulting concomitant variations, or covariations indicating theoretical generalizations. The different emphases of these two authors are not so much a problem, as an initial introduction to the broad variation in comparative analyses in anthropology. Comparison is used in many different ways by different anthropologists, and in different ways by the same anthropologists at different times. It has thus been shown to be capable of serving different theoretical premises and different objectives. Procedures of comparison vary according to the predilections of the authors. There is no one correct way to do comparative analysis; rather, comparison can be used in many ways to advance diverse anthropological purposes.

In the following chapters, four different strategies of comparison will be illustrated with well-known examples. Each example is placed in the category closest to its main orientation. But it is not uncommon for a study to combine different strategies, and we will see more than one in a number of examples.

- The first strategy is looking for the same pattern in different societies and different places. I call this a "type comparison." Here the author is looking for similar patterns in historically distinct cases.

- The second strategy is looking for different, contrasting patterns in different places. I call this "illustrative comparisons." The researcher is seeking cases markedly different from one another, to highlight the patterns in each.

- The third strategy is examining closely related communities, societies, and cultures, which share many common features and differ only in a few. I call this "controlled comparison." The anthropologist here attempts to find associated factors—concomitant relations—between two or more factors that vary together, being present in some cases and absent in others.

- The fourth strategy is examining all cases known of a particular type of society, or a representative sample of all cases. I call these "survey comparisons." The analyst seeks a reliable finding by including all possible cases, and by thus avoiding selection bias.

Both this division into four strategies and my labels for them are arbitrary, and could have been otherwise. But they should serve to introduce the richness of comparative analysis in anthropology.

Chapter Two

Type Comparisons

In type comparisons, the researcher is seeking the same customs, beliefs, or patterns of social relations in different places, in historically distinct societies. The objective is to identify various elements that go together in a regular fashion.

MOTHER'S BROTHER–SISTER'S SON RELATIONS

In many societies, the sister's son and mother's brother have a close and rather remarkable relationship, as defined by custom. Among the BaThonga of South Africa, the uncle looks after his uterine nephew with benevolent care. The uncle makes sacrifices when the nephew is sick. The uncle gracefully accepts many liberties on the part of the nephew; for example, the nephew can come to the uncle's house and eat any food prepared for the uncle. When the uncle sacrifices to his ancestors, the sister's son may take and consume the meat and beer offered to the gods. The nephew inherits some of the property of his mother's brother, and may sometimes claim one of his widows.

What is the reason for this very close and indulgent relationship? This is the question addressed by A. R. Radcliffe-Brown (1952) in a paper presented in South Africa in 1924. R-B doesn't much like the explanation offered by the ethnographer of the BaThonga, H. A. Junod, who says that this close relationship must be a hangover, or "'survival,'" of a previous matrilineal or matriarchal system, in which the sister's son was the inheritor and successor of the mother's brother. R-B objects that there is no evidence of a previous matrilineal system, so that positing it is mere conjecture, and that there are other features of the current

7

social relations that are not consistent with a previous matrilineal system. So R-B is intent on presenting an alternative explanation.

R-B begins with a type comparison, pointing out that similar customs guiding mother's brother–sister's son (MB–ZS) relations are found in other societies near and far. For example, among the Nama Hottentots, the ZS may take an especially fine animal from MB's herd, while the MB may take only deformed or decrepit beasts from ZS's herd. Yet more distant, on the Pacific Islands of Tonga and Fiji, certainly historically distinct from the African tribes, the ZS can take any of his maternal uncle's possessions, and eat the food that the MB sacrifices to the gods.

What the BaThonga, Nama, and Pacific Islanders of Tonga and Fiji have in common are patrilineal descent and patriarchal institutions. Children belong to their fathers' group, inherit through the male line, and succeed to office through the male line. The indulgent MB–ZS relationship is often found in patrilineal societies, and so is another, contrasting pattern: the strict, respectful relationship between father's sister (FZ) and brother's son (BS). FZ must always be respected and obeyed; FZ's word is law, and FZ is sacred to BS. This authoritarian FZ–BS relationship could not possibly be imagined as a residue of a previous matrilineal system, because the father's line has no authority in a matrilineal system. R-B further points out that the MB–ZS relationship and the FZ–BS relationship are not independent customs, varying without relation to one another, but rather are part of one system, the patrilineal system, and tend to go together. The two customs are present among the BaThonga, the Nama, and in Tonga and Fiji.

It is indicative for R-B that the mother's brother is called "male mother" in both South Africa and the Pacific Islands. Father's sister is called "female father," or "father's sister," or just "father." He sees the relationships with mother's kin as an extension of the relationship with mother, and the relationships with father's kin as an extension of the relationship with father. In turn, these relationships are defined by the system in place, in this case patrilineal and patriarchal, which assigns authority to the father's side and indulgence to the mother's. Thus the mother's brother–sister's son relationship is understandable as the appropriate nurturing and indulgence of the mother's side in the patrilineal system. Similarly, the strict, authoritarian father's sister–brother's son relationship reflects the hierarchy and responsibility of the kin group of which the boy is a junior member.

R-B, having through "type comparisons" established the connections between several different kin relationships, and their presence in several, dispersed societies, does touch on an "illustrative comparison" with societies having different patterns. One example is the Ila speakers of Northern Rhodesia, who have a matrilineal system. There the mother's brother is to sister's son the most powerful and greatest per-

son in the tribe; he has even the power of life and death ov
and nieces and must be respected above all. So relationships in ...
lineal groups appear to be the converse of those in patrilineal groups,
as one might expect. Furthermore, R-B points out that it is hard to see
how the authoritarian MB–ZS relationship in matrilineal systems
might morph into the indulgent MB–ZS relationship found in the patrilineal societies. Rather, the explanation is that group membership
determines relations. As R-B (1952:25) puts it:

> In primitive society there is a strongly marked tendency to merge
> the individual in the group to which he or she belongs. The result
> of this in relation to kinship is a tendency to extend to all the mem-
> bers of a group a certain type of behaviour which has its origin in a
> relationship to one particular member of the group. Thus the ten-
> dency in the BaThonga tribe would seem to be to extend to all the
> members of the mother's group (family or lineage) a certain pattern
> of behaviour which is derived from the special pattern that appears
> in the behaviour of a son towards his mother. Since it is from his
> mother that he expects care and indulgence he looks for the same
> sort of treatment from the people of his mother's group, i.e., from all
> his maternal kin. On the other hand it is to his paternal kin that he
> owes obedience and respect. The patterns that thus arise in rela-
> tion to the father and mother are generalised and extended to the
> kindred on the one side and on the other.

WHY CIVILIZATIONS DEVELOP

Some societies—Egyptian, Mesopotamian, and Incan—develop
over time ever more complex structures of technology and infrastruc-
ture and of social, cultural, economic, and political relations. There we
can find increasing dense populations and larger settlements, even
towns and cities, increased division of labor with specialized occupations and specialized technologies, and hierarchies both sacred and secular, commonly with specialized, often written languages. Other
societies—in much of East and Central Africa, in the Amazon—appear
to maintain a simpler, more basic structure, such as small village communities, reproducing themselves in stable continuity through time
and space. Specializations and hierarchies do not appear, nor does division of labor to any appreciable extent. Why is it that some societies
develop more and more complex forms, while others maintain their
basic, simple pattern?

Robert L. Carneiro (1961) attempts to answer this question by
exploring the nature of village communities of the Amazon basin. He
begins with an ethnographic account of the Kuikuru, a community of
some 145 souls living in nine large thatched houses, which appears to

be in many ways typical of the Amazon basin. It is a small community, with simple technology, largely slash and burn (swidden) horticulture, little division of labor beyond that of sex and age, little in the way of hierarchy or specialized institutions, and little in cultural development generally. The question discussed among Amazon specialists is why there is no more complex development. Most take the view that Amazonians are not able to develop further. Carneiro disagrees; he thinks that the Amazonians have no compelling reason to develop further.

One explanation advanced by anthropologists for why further development has not taken place in the Amazon is that the soils, weak in nutrients, cannot support ongoing cultivation, forcing inhabitants into a quasi-nomadic life. Carneiro points out that the Kuikuru have lived on virtually the same site for 90 years, and other Amazonian groups have been stable as well. Carneiro also reports agronomists' studies that confirm that the soils can be cultivated for ten years or more, with only modest reduction of crops. As well, it appears that the reason that Amazonians prefer to change fields (but not house sites) after three years is not that the fields are less productive, but that in successive years weeds intrude and require a much higher investment in labor. Amazonians are engaged in a calculus to minimize their labor input. Furthermore, Carneiro shows that Kuikuru manioc crops are hugely productive, requiring no more than two hours a day labor. This fact tends to undermine the argument, put forward by some specialists, that Amazonians cannot produce a surplus, which is necessary for higher levels of development. Carneiro argues that the Kuikuru could produce a large surplus, if they cared to do so, but they do not. He points out that when some groups of Amazonians were encouraged by the possibility of market sales, they produced large surpluses that they sold to white traders. Furthermore, the evidence suggests that cultivation, in the highly developed Inca area, was less productive per worker and per area than among the Kuikuru. So, Carneiro concludes, it was not that the Amazonians were incapable of further development, but that they were not inspired to undertake it.

How does Carneiro explain the cultural continuity of the Kuikuru, and their lack development initiative? Here he switches from type comparison to illustrative comparison, juxtaposing Amazonians with contrasting societies from elsewhere. He begins with Melanesia, another region traditionally dependent upon slash and burn horticulture. But things began to change as the population and the population density increased. More and more in some Melanesian societies, population began to outgrow the land available. This led them to intensify cultivation with various practices, in order to get more out of less land. Necessity of population pressure led to this change. In Amazonia, the population was so small, and the land area so vast, that the Kuikuru and others never had need to intensify cultivation; there was always fresh land available. Carneiro was thus able to identify population pressure as a main impetus for agricultural intensification and cultural development.

But Carneiro (1961:141) argues that population increase alone was not sufficient:

> Those regions where a notable intensification of agriculture followed an increase of population are distinguished by an important characteristic: *They are regions where the area of cultivable land was distinctly circumscribed.* Areas of distinctly circumscribed arable land are, typically, narrow valleys, sharply confined and delimited by mountains or deserts. It is in such areas that most of the early advances in agriculture, and in other aspects of culture, took place.

In such circumscribed areas, population pressures lead to competition for land, and then war for land. In large open regions, losers can move away. In circumscribed areas, the losers have nowhere to go, and must stay, often as subordinate to the winners. Need for land would lead to further conquest and political amalgamation. Successful military actors would gain rewards and eventually become a military class. Successful political leaders would become rulers of ever increasing domains, and an authority hierarchy would consolidate. A priestly class would likely emerge. Slave and drafted labor would be used for productive improvements, such as building terraces and cutting irrigation canals, and for civic improvement, such as building public buildings and roads, etc. Craft production would be stimulated, resulting in a class of specialists. Developments in ceramics, textiles, metallurgy, architecture, and so on, would result.

In both the Circum-Caribbean and the Andes more advanced cultural and political development, from chiefdoms to empires, were based on intensive agriculture in circumscribed areas, whether the coastal strips of Venezuela or the mountain valleys of Colombia, the coastal valleys of Peru or the inland river valleys. The Amazonians did not develop more complex forms of agriculture, politics, and culture because they were not forced to do so by population pressure, competition for land, warfare, and conquest. Those who lived in circumscribed regions, and whose population increased beyond capacity, enjoyed or suffered those pressures and their consequences in technical, cultural, and political development.

THE IMPACT OF THE MARKET

Similarities are sometimes found amidst diversity. Robert F. Murphy and Julian H. Steward found parallel developments in remarkably different places: among the Mundurucu tropical forest dwelling horticulturalists in Brazil, and among northeastern Algonkian nomadic hunters in subarctic Canada. Both groups, after contact with Europeans, were exposed to the international marketplace and commercial incentives and were transformed in similar ways. In their paper, "Tappers and Trappers: Parallel Process in Acculturation," Murphy and Steward (1956) begin by outlining the precontact patterns of the Mundurucu and Algonkians.

Northeast Algonkians, such as the Montagnais and the Naskapi were, prior to contact with whites, nomadic hunters who lived in small, informal bands that often split up in the winter as families pursued scattered game, such as deer and beaver, and families moved easily between bands, which were substantially unstructured. In the summer, fishing and hunting herd animals, such as caribou, allowed and encouraged larger bands to form, for group hunting works best with herd animals. With the arrival of white fur traders, trapping of fur-bearing animals, such as beaver, began to supplement hunting. However, the hunters soon became dependent on industrial goods, such as pots, pans, knives, axes, steel traps, and firearms, which were much more efficient than native products. What followed was a transition to greater dependency on fur trapping and fur trading, as men started leaving their families at the trading posts while they went to the bush to trap. Hunting declined in importance. Initially the band leader became a "chief" who mediated between the Indians and the white trader, but whose function was now limited to the trading post. Finally, the loose bands and collective cooperation and assistance in the bush were replaced by individual trappers with usufruct use rights to trapping territories. Although there were native agglomerations around trading post, the nuclear family became an independent socioeconomic unit, replacing the band.

The Mundurucu of Brazil lived deep inland in savannah lands and gallery forests, making a living primarily from slash and burn horticulture, mainly of manioc, and hunting and fishing. Each village was independent, putting the Mundurucu at the same level of sociocultural integration as the eastern Canadian Algonkians. But their village organization was stronger than that of the Algonkians, and their family organization weaker. In a practice not unusual in native South America, there were patrilineal moieties and clans, while families were matrilocal. What this meant in practice was that adult men lived in large, collective men's houses, and women and children had separate abodes. The men would visit the women to deliver game and fish, have sexual relations, and play with the children; in turn, the women would deliver cooked food to the men's house. Marriage ties were weak and easily broken. Game and fish were also distributed collectively, by the chief on behalf of the village, so everyone received a share and was secure in filling their needs.

When white traders came, they first bought mainly manioc flour, *farinha*. This was handled collectively by the villages; trading goods were distributed by the chief, who collected the flour and turned it over to the traders. When rubber became the traders' most desired product, this too was handled collectively by the village, the chief acting as the intermediary. But as the Mundurucu became increasingly dependent on traders' goods, and increasingly indebted to the traders, the traders appointed their own chief, the *capitao*, or captain, to control better the natives and the trading. At the same time, native warfare was being suppressed by the Brazilian government. These two developments undermined the traditional chiefs and the collective management of wealth, thus effectively destroying the indigenous political system. At the same time, increasing demand for rubber encouraged Mundurucu to devote more time to collecting rubber from the wild rubber trees among the rivers. This meant more time away from villages and less time devoted to horticulture. Permanent trading posts on rivers were established. The Mundurucu became increasingly dependent upon trading goods, and increasingly tied into trade through debt. As many Mundurucu became committed to full-time rubber collection, they moved permanently to their rubber tree groves, which were recognized as being under individual control. The Mundurucu economy, substantially collective in the villages, become individualized in the rubber groves. Unlike in the villages, family members lived together in dwellings, but different families lived distant from one another, each in their own grove. In the groves, family gardens were planted to provide food for the family. The trading post and the Catholic mission became the loci of such social life as remained.

There are parallel developments in both the Canadian Algonkians and the Brazilian Mundurucu. Both shifted, in gradual degrees, from subsistence production, production for use, to production for trade. They did so because they desired manufactured goods that traders brought. As Murphy and Steward (1956:351) put it:

> When goods manufactured by the industrialized nations with modern techniques become available through trade to aboriginal populations, the native people increasingly give up their homecrafts in order to devote their efforts to producing specialized cash crops or other trade items in order to obtain more of the industrially made articles.

The authors (1956:352–353) argue that this is a process of broad significance, affecting native populations worldwide, and that the consequences are no less than the undermining of native culture and the destruction of traditional societies.

> When the people of an unstratified native society barter wild products found in extensive distribution and obtained through individual effort, the structure of the native culture will be destroyed, and the

final culmination will be a culture-type characterized by individual
families having delimited rights to marketable resources and linked
to the larger nation through trading centers.

What about stratified native societies, or ones where wild products are
found in concentrated form and obtained through collective efforts? Is
the result the same? The authors switch into illustrative comparison
mode to explore a few contrasting cases. Trade on the Northwest Coast
of North America, with such groups as the Skagit and Bella Coola, who
had somewhat complex, multisettlement, stratified societies based on
the rich, concentrated resources of salmon, resulted in reinforcement of
the existing class system, intensified by the new wealth through elab-
orations on the potlatch competitions. At this higher level of sociocultural integration, given the wealth of wild products, trade reinforced
and intensified native society and culture, unlike among the eastern
Algonkians and Mundurucu, whose indigenous societies and cultures
were destroyed.

THE IDEOLOGY OF EQUALITY

People from apparently totally different social and cultural
milieux can, upon closer scrutiny, share important similarities. Such
is the case with the Inuit hunters of Port Burwell, Canada, and a New
Age population in the town of Glastonbury, in southwest England, discussed by David Riches in his article, "The Holistic Person; Or, The
Ideology of Egalitarianism" (2000).
    The Inuit of Port Burwell are a population of around 120 who have
gathered in a government-sponsored settlement. But they do not par-
ticipate in collective institutions such as the community council or
cooperative, which *faux de mieux* are run by Euro-Canadian officials,
because the hierarchical values inherent in these administrative structures violate Inuit norms of equality. A minority of Inuit have government jobs, and they bring in more money than others receive. But most
of this money is spent on hunting equipment—snowmobiles, canoes,
outboard engines—so that these employees can maintain their Inuit
cultural standing through participation in the paradigmatic Inuit
activity of hunting. Such well-equipped hunters often bring in more
game than others, which is a source of resentment, but everyone
expects the meat to be shared among all members of the community.
    The New Agers of Glastonbury, some 700 out of a population of
7,000, are mostly women, mainly of middle-class origins, well educated
in such fields as social work and teaching, usually young to middle-
aged. They tend not to pursue occupational achievement, in a way have
"dropped out," and are viewed as unproductive by some outsiders. They

hold a moral commitment to equality and distributive justice, and while they do not share income, they do provide building, cleaning, care, craft, technical, and health services to others according to need, with the goals of social mutuality, unreserved friendship, and love.

The concept of equality advocated by the Inuit and New Agers is equality of outcome, in which everyone ends up in more or less the same position. This contrasts with a more limited concept of equality, equality of opportunity, held by "mainstream" culture in industrialized societies, in which everyone gets a chance, but outcomes will vary according to capability, effort, and luck. Equality of outcome, however attractive, contains, according to Riches (2000:671, 676), an inevitable, internal contradiction:

> On the one hand, this egalitarianism hinders the development of political authority; on the other hand, weak political authority leaves the individual relatively immune to levelling-out edicts. In short, egalitarianism legitimates autonomy, which subverts egalitarianism. . . . This contradiction exemplifies a social process whereby a moral notion is confounded by the individual action that it legitimates.

In other words, political control of people's behavior to insure equality requires a political hierarchy, a coercive hierarchy, which itself is offensive to egalitarian ideals. However, without this hierarchical coercion, people are free to do as they like, and this results in different outcomes of wealth or prestige for different people, undermining the ideal of equality of outcome. So if people hold the ideal of equality of outcome, but allow freedom for individuals to act independently and bring about different, unequal outcomes, how do people reconcile the ideal with the reality? This is the central question that Riches addresses.

Both the Inuit and the New Agers believe that the person is made up of diverse elements: the Inuit person incorporates body, soul, name (knowledge), and breath (sociality); the New Age person is indissolubly spiritual, mental, emotional (intuitive), and physical. Riches (2000:677) calls this concept of the person "the holistic person."

> I interpret the holistic person as a discourse on individual moral frailty, because it celebrates balance with regard to the multiple elements that constitute the human being. . . . [But] such balance, because it refers to disparate elements, can be lost easily. The result is that the person has a reduced capacity directly to determine the outcome of events. . . . The point of the discourse is that actions that depart from moral expectation are deemed to be inevitable, and to be experienced with relative equanimity.

Furthermore, because people are connected to wider systems of physical forces, spirit forces, deceased relatives, and previous lives, they are subject to pressures from beyond themselves that can throw them out of balance, which leads people to follow unideal courses. It is believed by the Inuit and New Agers that people often cannot help falling out of balance, and so their deviant behavior must be viewed with tolerance and acceptance. In this way, the concept of the holistic person mediates between ideals and unideal behaviors, thus "transcending the two parts of the contradiction" (Riches 2000:677). The concept of the holistic person allows people to hold their ideals and maintain their community in spite of the unideal behaviors of some members. This concept is thus a form of ideological lubrication, allowing somewhat incompatible parts to continue to operate together, and by so doing, thus maintaining the ideals and the deviant behaviors as they are.

SUMMARY

We have seen how R-B finds the indulgent MB–ZS relationship replicated in a range of patrilineal societies, Carneiro sees circum-scribed populations around the world tending toward complex develop-ment, Murphy and Steward find engagement with Western trade leading diverse peoples along convergent trajectories, and Riches dis-covers common ideas as contrasting societies seek to resolve the contra-diction between the ideals and realities of egalitarianism. Type comparisons, showing the presence of particular patterns in a range of historically unrelated cultures, provide a firm foundation for general knowledge about these otherwise puzzling patterns.

Chapter Three

Illustrative Comparisons

In illustrative comparisons, the researcher is seeking contrasting customs, beliefs, or patterns of social relations in different places, in historically distinct or related societies. The objective is to show differences, and to consider why the differences exist.

PATTERNS OF CULTURE

People are capable of many different things. Peoples tend, in their ways of life, to do things differently from one another. Anthropologists call a people's way of life their culture. Ruth Benedict, one of the founders of American anthropology, in her influential volume, *Patterns of Culture* (1935[1934]), showed that placement on the "Great Arc of Culture" determined what a people's customs and lives would be like.

> In culture . . . we must imagine a great arc on which are ranged the possible interests provided either by the human age-cycle or by the environment or by man's various activities. . . . Identity as a culture depends upon the selection of some segment of this arc. Every human society has made such a selection in its cultural institutions (Benedict 1935[1934]:17).

Thus different peoples, each emphasizing different aspects of life, have different customs and different lives.

What people in a particular culture aim for, think about, worry about, and hope for, according to Benedict, depends on the theme of their culture. Culture is not a random collection of "shreds and patches," as some earlier anthropologists had suggested, thinking of the diffusion of cultural elements through borrowing. Rather, Benedict

(1935[1934]:33) argues, culture is a *gestalt,* a pattern in which all of the elements conform to a determining theme.

> A culture . . . is a more or less consistent pattern of thought and action. Within each culture there come into being characteristic purposes not necessarily shared by other types of society. In obedience to these purposes, . . . items of behavior take more and more congruous shape.

Thus each culture has a kind of spirit to which all customs and behaviors are oriented. Benedict famously illustrates her approach by examining three distinctly different cultures: the Zuni Pueblos, the Dobu, and the Northwest Coast Indians.

The Zuni are former cliff dwellers who live along the Rio Grande in New Mexico. Benedict characterizes the Zuni with Nietzsche's label "Apollonian" (after Apollo, the Greek & Roman god of light, healing, music, poetry, and prophecy): an approach that stresses moderation, order, and calm, and avoids intense emotions and disruptive psychological states. Tradition is the great guide for Apollonians, in opposition to individualism, innovation, and spontaneity, which must be suppressed. As Benedict (1935[1934]:42) says:

> The Zuni are a ceremonious people, a people who value sobriety and inoffensiveness above all other virtues. Their interest is centred upon their rich and complex ceremonial life. Their cults of the masked gods, of healing, of the sun, of the sacred fetishes, of war, of the dead, are formal and established bodies of ritual with priestly officials and calendric observances. No field of activity competes with ritual for foremost place in their attention. Probably most grown men among the western Pueblos give to it the greater part of their waking life.

The Zuni make a living in their generous environment from gardens, orchards, flocks, and silver and turquoise, with no special trouble or attention. Family life is informal and flexible; even marriage and divorce are individual and placid. Benedict says that "Everyday in Zuni there are fresh instances of their mildness" (Benedict 1935[1934]:76). All of Zuni focus and attention is concentrated on ritual; "no other aspect of existence seriously competes in Zuni interest with the dances and the religious observances" (52).

Nietzsche contrasts the Apollonian with the Dionysian (after Dionysus, the Greek god of fertility, wine, and drama), an emphasis on intensity, excess, and surpassing ordinary boundaries of the self and the limits of existence. Benedict argues that almost all Native American cultures, other than the Pueblo, are Dionysian, in which individuals strive, through drugs, self-mutilation, alcohol, fasting, or risk of injury or death, to go beyond their quotidian selves and touch the gods, the universe, and the grounds of existence. Typically, there is a striving for a dream-vision from which, it is believed, comes supernatural power. The peoples of the Great Plains were exemplary in their Dionysian extremes.

The second people that Benedict describes is the Dobu of Melanesia, living on an island close by the Trobriand Islands made famous in the work of Bronislaw Malinowski. The Dobuans appear to have selected out of all possible characteristics to emphasize: fear, animosity, and malignancy. While these exist to some degree in all human experience, in Dobu they are the central features and are valued rather than disparaged. As Benedict (1935[1934]:94) puts it:

> The Dobuans . . . are lawless and treacherous. Every man's hand is against every other man. . . . Dobu put a premium upon ill-will and treachery and make of them recognized virtues of their society.

Threat comes within one's own community, the locality of up to 20 villages, from witches and sorcerers who daily attempt to attack. Threat comes from outside of the locality by means of raids and warfare. Among the other islands, Dobuans were infamous for raiding, sorcery, and cannibalism. Doubuan married couples are divided by the hostility between their matrilines, expected sexual infidelity, fear of theft of yam lines and gardens, and possible sorcery or poisoning. In interisland trade of the Kula Ring, Dobuans try to cheat their partners and gain the maximum with false promises. Success in yam production, sex, trade, health, property, sailing, and combat all depend upon magical incantations, which themselves are malicious, as in gaining health by sending disease to another, or growing yams by magically taking them from another garden. Benedict (1935[1934]:102) sums up the Dobuan attitude: In Dobu

> all existence is cut-throat competition, and every advantage is gained at the expense of a defeated rival. This competition . . . is secret and treacherous. The good man, the successful man, is he who has cheated another of his place.

There is no law and no legitimate authority on Dobu. Everything is left to individuals and their small matrikin as they face off against other individuals and matrikin. All relationships outside of the matrikin are based on aggression, acting and imposing what you will and what you can. There are no constraining social institutions. Shockingly,

> the Dobuan lives out without repression man's worst nightmares of the ill-will of the universe, and according to his view of life virtue consists in selecting a victim upon whom he can vent the malignancy he attributes alike to human society and the powers of nature. All existence appears to him as a cut-throat struggle in which deadly antagonists are pitted against one another in a contest for each one of the goods of life. Suspicion and cruelty are his trusted weapons in the strife and he gives no mercy, and he asks none. (Benedict 1935[1934]:124)

In Dobu, paranoia is realism, and maliciousness is virtue. Life as a nightmare is life on Dobu.

Benedict's third case is one of the Dionysian peoples: the tribes of the Northwest Coast, in particular the Kwakiutl. The Northwest Coast is one of the world's richest natural environments, overflowing with animals and plants of many, many useful types. Great prosperity is gained with very modest effort. Much time and energy is invested in cultural elaboration, such as the magnificent woodworking of houses, canoes, and totem poles, and the mats, baskets, blankets, and etched copper sheets. But all of these practical items were often used for ritual purposes, as we shall see shortly. Kwakiutl religious ceremonies strove for ecstasy. Dancers would engage in violent and abnormal behaviors, from going into a trance, to cannibalism of corpses or taking bites from onlookers, to contact with menstrual blood, all in aid of rising to divine madness that gave one supernatural powers.

Northwest Coast tribes were solidary groups, owning hunting and fishing rights in common. These tribes were also hierarchical, with hierarchy defined by inherited names, myths, songs, privileges, and related house posts, spoons, and heraldic crests, all of which could be owned only by individuals. Titles were inherited by seniority, through the female line.

> The ultimate reason why a man of the North-West Coast cared about the nobility titles, the wealth, the crests and the prerogatives lays bare the mainspring of their culture: they used them in a contest in which they sought to shame their rivals. (Benedict 1935[1934]:136)

Returning now to all of the lovely, practical goods produced in this rich land, many were destined not to be used in ordinary life but rather to be given away or to be destroyed in a political competition, called "potlatch." The point of a potlatch was to shame a rival, who was one's guest at a banquet, by giving or destroying more than the rival could reciprocate. "They say, 'We do not fight with weapons. We fight with property'" (Benedict 1935[1934]:136).

> The object of all Kwakiutl enterprise was to show oneself superior to one's rivals. This will to superiority they exhibited in the most uninhibited fashion. It found expression in uncensored self-glorification and ridicule of all comers ... unabashed megalomania. (Benedict 1935[1934]:137)

For example, a song sung by chief's retainers at such competitions:

> I am the great chief who makes people ashamed.
>
> I am the great chief who makes people ashamed.
>
> Our chief brings shame to the faces.
>
> Our chief brings shame to the faces.
>
> Our chief brings jealousy.
>
> Our chief brings jealousy. . . .

For the Kwakiutl, "all the motivations they recognized centred around the will to superiority. . . . The whole economic system of the North-West Coast was bent to the service of this obsession" (Benedict 1935[1934]:138–139). The ideal man is one who achieves superiority over all rivals, shaming and humiliating them, triumphing over all.

Ruth Benedict wanted to convey three lessons in *Patterns of Culture*. First, cultures are different from one another. They are based on different aspects of life that serve as their themes. Thus different cultures are noncommensurable. People whose lives are informed by one culture see the world differently from those with another culture. Each culture therefore has to be understood in its own terms. This is one of the basic tenets of "cultural relativism." Now, thanks partly to Benedict, this is all well-known and broadly accepted; as Clifford Geertz has said, "culture" is now out in the streets, that is, the idea of culture and cultural relativism is general knowledge.

Second, cultures are not random collections of customs, ideas, values, and practices. Rather, each culture is formed into a pattern, a configuration, based on a central idea. That is, culture has a particular spirit to which all of its parts are assimilated. In this way, a culture is coherent, a unity, all of a piece. People are not pulled in all directions by their culture, made schizophrenic or pluro-schizophrenic, but rather guided along one clear path.

Third, because we are creatures of our own cultures, we should be tolerant of those from other cultures, and furthermore recognize that our own culture, being somewhat arbitrary, should accept with tolerance its own deviants. This advice is of course moral advice, not scientific theory or hypothesis such as the first two conclusions.

Benedict's first conclusion about the diversity of cultures is the most basic principle of anthropology and has been almost universally appreciated in our global society. Her third conclusion advising tolerance of other cultures and other peoples has been widely adopted in the West as "multiculturalism," although labeled by those less enthusiastic as "political correctness." Recently this third principle of tolerance of other cultures has begun to impinge on Benedict's first principle about the diversity of cultures. Increasingly, at least in the West, it is regarded as incorrect to speak of differences of culture, presumably on the ground that any comparison is invidious, implying superiority and inferiority. We speak of "diversity," but do not like to talk about differences. Even anthropologists have begun to shy away from discussing cultural differences, replacing such discussion with informants' "stories" about themselves.

Benedict's second conclusion, asserting the coherence of each culture, the unity of its vision, and the purity of its spirit, is also challenged, or as we say today, "contested," by those of a postmodern bent as an oversimplified reification or, alternatively, reductionism, of the diversity, plurality, and multivocality of each culture, which in the post-modern view makes a culture virtually undescribable. For this reason some students of culture have given up attempts at scientific or even descriptive accounts of cultures and in their stead have devoted themselves to moral and political advocacy.

There is an intermediate position, between the strong version of Benedict's conclusion that each culture is fully integrated and the postmodern view that cultures are so diverse as not to be identifiable. The intermediate position would say, first, that some cultures are highly integrated, while others are less so. This point was in fact acknowledged by Benedict, who even gave some examples of poorly integrated cultures. A second point would be that all members of a culture are not equally in tune with the theme of the culture, as some personalities would fit well with a culture and others not so well. Again, Benedict also made this point, providing as an example a strong-willed, assertive Zuni who bridled under the necessary restraint of Zuni social life. So Benedict clearly understood the variation and diversity of personality types in any population and thus in any culture. Finally, the third view of an intermediate position would be that, even if a culture is not entirely integrated around a theme, we must recognize that all description and all knowledge are based on abstraction and generalization, and that diversity does not invalidate the observation of general tendencies. Our categories and their labels, such as "tree," mask a great range of different types, and still can be validly distinguished from "grass," of which there are also many types, and from "rocks," etc. etc. Similarly, "tribal" cultures, notwithstanding their great diversity, are quite different from "agrarian" cultures, and both are validly differentiated from "industrial" cultures, and so on. Individual cultures too—French, Iranian, Thai, etc., etc.—are equally validly distinguished from one another, although each has noteworthy regional and other variations.

At the very least, Benedict's emphasis on cultural integration can inspire us to investigate the extent to which any particular culture, any specific type of culture, or cultures in general are integrated. In this way, our conclusions will not be based on first principles, as both Benedict's strong formulation and the postmodern rejection are, but on evidence resulting from study and analytic assessment. With this proviso, the credit goes to Benedict.

OPEN AND CLOSED COMMUNITIES

An emphasis on solidarity and unity is typical of corporate communities. A well-known example is the "corporate" village of highland Latin America, so labeled and described in Eric Wolf's 1955 paper,

"Types of Latin American Peasantry." Members lived in a "bounded social system with clear-cut limits, in relations to both outsiders and insiders" (Wolf 1955:456). Community members were co-owners of their land and participated in communal political and religious affairs. Land was often reallocated every year, and it was forbidden to sell it to outsiders. Prestige and power were based on community decisions and involved "rising from religious office to office along a prescribed ladder of achievement" (Wolf 1955:458). From these processes a sense of solidarity developed, for with resources flowing into community institutions, conspicuous consumption by individuals was precluded. Thus "the *political-religious system* as a whole tend[ed] to define the boundaries of the community and act[ed] as a rallying point and symbol of collective unity." And this inward-looking unity was further supported by the marriage pattern, which was endogamous, that is, people married other members of the home community rather than with outsiders. Co-ownership of land and coparticipation in political and religious decisions maintained equality. In this way, "The corporate structure act[ed] to impede the mobilization of capital and wealth within the community in terms of the outside world which employ[ed] wealth capitalistically" (Wolf 1955:458). The consequence was economic equalization:

> The community at one and the same time levels differences of wealth which might intensify class divisions within the community to the detriment of the corporate structure and symbolically reasserts the strength and integrity of its structure before the eyes of its members. (Wolf 1955:458)

The other side of the corporate peasant community was restriction on individual autonomy and freedom. As Wolf says, "Seen from within, [the corporate community] defines the rights and duties of its members and prescribes large segments of their behavior" (Wolf 1955:456). There is a culturally recognized standard of consumption that consciously excludes cultural alternatives. "By reducing alternative items of consumption, along with the kinds of behavior and ideal norms which make use of these items of consumption, the community reduces the threat to its integrity" (Wolf 1955:458–459). Any sign of behavior threatening the equality of community members—behavior such as conspicuous show of individual wealth, abuse of power, or economic mobility—would be met by the well-established control mechanism of institutionalized envy, in such manifestations as gossip, attacks of the evil eye, and witchcraft. Community members could not accumulate land or wealth, could not consume items beyond the conventional repertoire, and could not marry beyond community boundaries. Thus we find that in these corporate peasant communities economic equality was firmly established and rigorously defended by suppressing individual freedom and autonomy. Equality was achieved, but at the cost of individual liberty and autonomy.

What Wolf called "open" peasant communities, which he described as typifying Latin America's humid low highlands and tropical lowlands, were, as he specified, producers of cash crops that constituted around 50 to 75 percent of their total production. Peasants there relied on the world market to absorb agricultural products, and they suffered and benefited from cyclical fluctuations in demand. In their turn, these peasants, often of European origin, desired consumption goods from the market, not least prestige goods that would raise their status:

> Status behavior is loaded with a fierce consciousness of the symbols of status, while "redefining" behavior aims at testing the social limits [with others]. The most important of these types of behavior consists in the ostentatious exhibition of commodities purchased with money. (Wolf 1955:461–462)

In these open communities was found an interplay between economic inequality and differentiation of status, with inequality making differentiation possible, and with status differentiation motivating economic striving. This process was exacerbated by informal alliances of families and clients that polarized wealth and power. "Participation in a complex system of hierarchical relationships and prestige required the consumption of goods that could be produced only by means of a complicated division of labor and had to be acquired in the market" (Wolf 1955:461–462). Competition for wealth and status both reflected and generated differentiation between families, which in turn reduced solidarity among community members:

> Such accumulation of goods and the behavior associated with it serves as a challenge to existing relations with kin folk, both real and fictitious, since it is usually associated with a reduction in relations of reciprocal aid and hospitality on which these ties are based. (Wolf 1955:466)

The economic differentiation and lack of solidarity found in "open" peasant communities were associated with individual and family autonomy and the freedom to make one's own decisions as one saw fit. This was possible because land, the most important capital resource, was owned privately rather than collectively and could be mortgaged or pawned for capital according to the decisions of individual families. Likewise, decisions about crops grown and market products purchased were up to each family individually. The wider community could not interfere in such decisions. Freedom of association could be seen in ties between peasants and outsiders, who often acted as business partners or patrons.

Thus, in the open peasant communities of Latin America we see a reversed pattern in relation to that of the corporate peasant community. Whereas the corporate peasant community negated individual freedom in favor of economic equality and community solidarity, the open peasant community negated economic equality in favor of individual freedom and worldly success.

TOTEM AND CASTE

Distinct cultures can be examined to find their dominant patterns, and juxtaposed to illuminate their differences, as Benedict does, or they can be shown to be parts of different economic systems, as Wolf does with Latin American communities. Another approach to comparison is to seek the underlying principles of organization of distinct cultures, the "deep structure," and to show how remarkably contrasting cultures can be seen as simple transformations of one another's principles. This Lévi-Strauss does in *The Savage Mind* (1966) with Australian totemic organization and South Asian caste.

"Both the exchange of women and the exchange of food are means of securing or of displaying the interlocking of social groups with one another." So L-S (1966:109) begins chapter 4 of *The Savage Mind*. L-S is not an ethnographer, reporting in detail his own research on a particular people. Rather, he is a synthesizer and theorist, and *The Savage Mind*, like his other works, is rife with illustrative comparisons drawn from the ethnographic and historical literature. The first issue that L-S raises in this chapter is whether the exchange of women and food are separate or go in different directions, and so balance one another, or both go in the same direction, which L-S called "accumulation." He contrasts this activity as practiced on the island of Dobu in Melanesia with how it is practiced in Australia. In Dobu, exogamy is the rule, but along with fear and loathing of the malicious and dangerous outsiders into whom one marries; exogamy there goes along with endo-agriculture, in which each husband and each wife own their own yam seeds and each gardens separately. Thus on Dobu exogamy binds groups together, no matter how unwillingly, while endo-agriculture expresses the hostility between groups. In Australia, on the other hand, both food and women, in "accumulation," bind groups together. Totemic clans are exogamous, and the food prohibition and rituals practiced in a clan for the clan totem are thought to increase the numbers of the totemic animal for the benefit of the other clans.

L-S argues that in full totemic systems, the relations between clans and their totems are really the relation between the differences between natural species totems—e.g., snake is to rabbit is to bird is to rat—and the posited differences between clans—clan A is to clan B is to clan C is to clan D—rather than the individual connections between clan A and snake, clan B and rabbit, and so on.

> When nature and culture are thought of as two systems of differences between which there is a formal analogy . . . social groups are distinguished from one another but they retain their solidarity as parts of the same whole, and the rule of exogamy furnishes the means of resolving this opposition balanced between diversity and unity. (1966:116)

However, if the conceptual focus is not two parallel sets of differences, but instead is the relations between each group and its totem, that tends to undermine the unity between groups. L-S (1966:116) explains:

> If social groups are considered not so much from the point of view of their reciprocal relations in social life as each on their own account. . . . Each social group will tend to form a system no longer with other groups but with particular differentiating properties regarded as hereditary, and these characteristics exclusive to each group will weaken the framework of their solidarity within the society.

An example (L-S 1966:118) from the Chickasaw Indians illustrates:

> The Raccoon people were said to live on fish and wild fruit, those of the Puma lived in the mountains, avoided water of which they were very frightened and lived principally on game. The Wild Cat clan slept in the daytime and hunted at night, for they had keen eyes. . . . Members of the Bird clan were up before day-break.

And so on with the Red Fox people and the others, each thought to have very particular characteristics that differentiated them from all other clans. These societies, according to L-S, are conceived of as having castes arising from nature. Such groups are conceptually intermediate between totemic groups and full castes. This shift marks the "conceptual passage from exogamy to endogamy (or vice versa)" (L-S 1966:117).

Castes in South Asia are occupationally specialized, each contributing to the others its necessary goods and services. Because these services are real, exist in the material world, they do not need to be duplicated by the exchange of women between groups. As L-S (1966:125) puts it, "Castes are heterogeneous in function and can therefore be homogeneous in structure." In fact, the cultural differences in occupation have been conceived as hereditary and natural, each caste a kind of natural species in which its members are naturally different from those in other castes, and therefore exchange of women between castes is forbidden. In contrast, totemic groups are in practice homogeneous in functions, because their ritual does not really increase their totemic species, so they must be heterogeneous in structure, defining their women as different social species and exchanging them. Thus women can be conceived as naturally different, so they cannot be exchanged, a view which is tied to endogamy, or they can be conceived as alike, so they can be exchanged, a view tied to exogamy. As L-S (1966:124) says, "Castes decree women to be naturally heterogeneous; totemic groups decree them to be culturally heterogeneous." L-S (1966:127) sums up:

> Castes picture themselves as natural species while totemic groups picture natural species as castes. And this must be refined: castes naturalize a true culture falsely, totemic groups culturalize a false nature truly.

In spite of these differences, both totemic groups and occupational castes are "exopracticing," the former through the exchange of women, the latter through the exchange of goods. In both cases, groups are tied together into a larger unity.

But there is more to these systems than social solidarity. They must also resolve the conceptual relation of nature and culture, a major theme in L-S's work. L-S (1966:127) argues that "the system of natural species and that of manufactured objects [are] two mediating sets which man employs to overcome the opposition between nature and culture and think of them as a whole." But they do not have to do their work alone: the "system of women" serves as a middle term between natural species and manufactured objects, integrating them into a unified group.

ISLAM OBSERVED

Within overarching civilizations, such as Islam, even under pressure for uniformity, there are many variations, often arising from particular local and regional conditions and circumstances. As well, a tradition and a wider culture do not remain fixed over time, but change and evolve. In his short book, *Islam Observed* (1968), Clifford Geertz undertakes, based in part on his ethnographic field research in the two countries, a comparison between Indonesian Islam and Moroccan Islam. As well, Geertz compares the development of the two traditions, considering them during their classical, scripturalist, and modern periods. This ambitious double comparison—across cultures and through time—is a daunting exercise. As Geertz (1968:v) says, "Merely to state such a program is to demonstrate a certain lack of grasp upon reality. What results can only be too abbreviated to be balanced and too speculative to be demonstrable." And yet Geertz's comparisons appear to be brilliant to many readers.

Moroccan and Indonesian environments and societies were and are markedly different. Morocco is an arid land of mountains and deserts, with the plain along the Mediterranean being its mildest area. Indonesia is a humid tropical land, rich with ancient volcanic soils. Correspondingly, Moroccan mountains and deserts were occupied by tribal peoples engaged in raising livestock and in marginal cultivation, with only the coastal plain suitable for productive agriculture. The Indonesian heartland, in contrast, was densely occupied by a highly productive wet rice farming peasantry.

In Morocco, the tribes were constantly intruding on the coastal plain and in the coastal cities:

> The formative period both of Morocco as a nation and of Islam as its creed (roughly 1050 to 1450) consisted of the peculiar process of tribal edges falling in upon an agricultural center and civilizing it. It was the periphery of the country, the harsh and sterile frontiers, that nourished and in fact created the advanced society which developed at its heart. (Geertz 1968:5)

Rural and urban Morocco shared the same culture but lived it in different circumstances. Rural-urban interaction, both congenial and conflictful, was "the central dynamic of historical change in Morocco" (Geertz 1968:7). The spirit of Moroccan culture was that of the tribes. "It is out of the tribes that the forming impulses of Islamic civilization in Morocco came, and the stamp of their mentality remained on it" (Geertz 1968:9). The basic style, or, one might say, spirit of Moroccan life

> was about everywhere the same: strenuous, fluid, violent, visionary, devout, and unsentimental, but above all, self-assertive. It was a society in which a very great deal turned on force of character and most of the rest on spiritual reputation. . . . The axial figure, whether he was storming walls or building them, was the warrior saint. (Geertz 1968:8)

Whether in Fez and Marrakech, or in the high Atlas, or the Sahara, Moroccan Islam was an Islam of "saint worship and moral severity, magical power and aggressive piety" (Geertz 1968:9).

> The approach developed was one of uncompromising rigorism. . . . Moroccan Islamism came over the centuries to embody a marked strain of religious and moral perfectionism, a persisting determination to establish a purified, canonical, and completely uniform creed. (Geertz 1968:16)

In contrast to Morocco's tribal society, Indonesia, especially Java, was basically a peasant society. The model individual was not the striving, assertive tribesman awaiting his chance to impose his will, but rather the

> settled, industrious, rather inward plowman of twenty centuries, nursing his terrace, placating his neighbors, and feeding his superiors. In Morocco civilization was built on nerve; in Indonesia, on diligence. (Geertz 1968:11)

The Indonesian approach to Islam was in the same spirit: "adaptive, absorbent, pragmatic, and gradualistic, a matter of partial compromises, half-way covenants, and outright evasions" (Geertz 1968:16).

There is more to the difference between Morocco and Indonesia than environment and making a living. Morocco was occupied largely by tribal Berbers before the invasion by Arab tribesmen. There was a structural similarity between the invaders and the natives that allowed continuity in the unfettered development of tribally inspired Islam. Particularly noteworthy is the incorporation in Moroccan Islam of the two central tribal principles: one is descent, which is the basis of lineages, clans, and tribes, and the other is achievement. Descent from the Prophet became a major source of religious and thus political legitimacy. Personal religious power, conceived as *baraka*, or supernatural abilities, was the other source of religious and political legitimacy. Saints were those who had proven their baraka, and their descendants, drawing on the first principle, were deemed to have inherited some of their holy ancestor's baraka.

The Indonesia, especially Java, that received Islam, had a highly developed Indic civilization. Hindu-Buddhist influences shaped the Javanese states, each manifesting elaborate political, aesthetic, religious, and social arrangements. These "theater states" did not so much govern, as exemplified through its rituals the values of Javanese culture. Furthermore, when Islam did come to Indonesia, it came via traders, rather than tribal conquerors, and it came from India rather than from Arabia. The result was that Indonesian Islam took on much of the spirit of Indic Javanese culture.

In sum, Islam in Indonesia and Morocco were manifest in quite different spirits:

> On the Indonesian side, inwardness, imperturbability, patience, poise, sensibility, aestheticism, elitism, and an almost obsessive self-effacement, the radical dissolution of individuality; on the Moroccan side, activism, fervor, impetuosity, nerve, toughness, moralism, populism, and individuality. (Geertz 1968:54)

Geertz is thus able to show, with many examples and details that cannot be included here, that even a tradition apparently as specific and coherent as Islam can be manifested in different cultural contexts in quite different ways. Also illustrated by this comparison is more specifically the way in which particular cultures shape a tradition such as Islam into regionally and locally relevant forms.

FARMERS AND PASTORALISTS

Many anthropologists compare "natural" units, that is entities that exist in their own right: groups, communities, societies, cultures, civilizations. But it is also possible to compare analytic categories, that is, types defined by specific criteria, e.g., rural vs. urban, hunter vs. gatherer, or rich vs. poor. Radcliffe-Brown, in the paper discussed above, takes this approach in comparing patrilineal vs. matrilineal kinship systems. Note that all of these example cases that fall in one or the other category may come from a wide range of cultures and societies. There is no "stand alone" patrilineal kinship system, or urban life, or capitalism; all are found in different social and cultural contexts. Each analytic category is defined by certain criteria, and the contrast between the two (or more) categories is a result of the definitions. Note that defining categories tells us only how we intend to use terms and concepts; it tells us nothing about the world. However, when we examine the world using those categories, we might, if the categories capture something important about reality, discover that various other characteristics are associated with those we have defined analytically, and thus learn things about the way the world works. In other words, our analytic categories are proved valid if they are fruitful in reliably indicating related qualities. If we find that urbanites around the world are more dependent and more tolerant, while rural folk are more independent and more judgmental, we have discovered a consistent human pattern.

This is the goal of Robert Edgerton in *The Individual in Cultural Adaptation: A Study of Four East African Peoples* (1971). The title is slightly misleading, because he is not only studying four East African peoples but is also studying farmers and pastoralists in those societies: the Hehe of Tanzania, the Kamba and Pokot of Kenya, and the Sebei of Uganda. His objective is not only to understand the unique qualities of each of the four cultures but also to discover the common characteristics of farmers and pastoralists in the four societies. This is made possible because each society has both farmers and pastoralists. By looking at members of these categories across the four societies, Edgerton hopes to factor out, to "control," the unique influences of particular cultures in order to abstract the features of farming and pastoralism that shape values, beliefs, attitudes, and sentiments. In his final conclusions, Edgerton presents only those contrasts between farmers and pastoralists that exist in all four societies.

Edgerton's study is inspired by a cultural ecological approach. To quote from Walter Goldschmidt's (1971:5) "Introduction" to the Edgerton volume:

> A theory of cultural ecology postulates that, as the external situation varies, the effective instrumentation in the form of tools and techniques also varies and the requirements for effective human collaboration are altered, and that, therefore, it is possible and often necessary for *institutions* to take on different forms and hence for *individual behavior* to change in conformity if it is to be appropriate to the new situation.

Edgerton, as a student of human psychology, is particularly interested in mental and psychological processes and characteristics, and how they play a role in society and culture, and in ecology. Edgerton (1971:24) specifies that

> our presumption, then, was not that values, attitudes, and personality attributes were epiphenomena of the essential social and cultural processes that stood at the core of an ecosystem, but rather that they were part and parcel of the system itself.

Edgerton in this work reports research conducted on the cultural and psychological attributes of farmers and pastoralists. Of course, the findings are limited to East African farmers and pastoralists, based as they are on the kinds of farmers and pastoralists found in East Africa: unmounted herders maintaining cattle as a primary objective, augmented by sheep and goats; and farmers cultivating without plow and draft animals, as Goldschmidt (in Edgerton 1971:9) specifies. But Edgerton's findings are at the very least suggestive, and thus are the basis for hypotheses about farmers and pastoralists elsewhere.

Unlike most cultural anthropologists who rely on "participant observation," living in situ with the people being studied, observing events, and speaking with "informants," Edgerton employs a battery of psychological tests, supplemented by observation. His choice of tests, pretesting, and final selection are outlined in his lengthy chapter 1, "Procedures and Methods: Collection and Coding of the Data." His final set of tools included an open-ended interview using 85 questions; ten Rorschach (ink blot) cards; nine "values pictures," drawings of people in somewhat ambiguous attitudes and activities; and 22 color slides of people and scenes, some from East Africa. A sample of individuals from the populations studied, totaling 505 individuals, was selected and engaged with these tests. All four of these tools could be considered projective tests, because they offer the respondent an "ambiguous stimulus" that elicits the respondent's own ideas, thoughts, feelings, and attitudes. Edgerton also discusses the procedures for coding the data, that is, deciding what an answer means, so that it can be placed in the correct category. Finally, Edgerton (1971:69–70) discusses the validity of the findings, and concludes that

> the strength of these data is their objectivity and comparability. Our primary goal . . . was to collect comparable data from eight dis-

tinct populations [farmers and herders in the four societies]. In at-
tempting to achieve this goal, a concession had to be made. That
concession was in favor of objectivity and comparability, and it produced data that were relatively reduced in complexity, subtlety,
and personal involvement.

And yet, the findings are not only more precise, but also more complex
and subtle than many conventional ethnographic accounts.

Edgerton's ethnographic descriptions, while brief and far from
comprehensive, are suggestive. Here (1971:93–94) is a passage about
the Hehe farmers:

> The farming neighborhood of Ngelewala was quiet. . . . The lack of
> bustle and noise came in part from the great dispersion of home-
> steads. No matter where one stood, the houses of these Hehe farmers
> remained hidden from view by their wide separation, their distance
> from the walking paths, and by the fringe of trees and crops that sur-
> rounded them. Much was hidden within these houses, too, for these
> massive, thick walled enclosures seemed to stand as fortresses sep-
> arating their occupants from the world outside. The people of
> Ngelewala were also hidden from view. The people were small in
> stature, graceful, and dignified, but they were not often in evidence.
> What was equally significant, when they did meet each other, they
> continued to hide, this time behind a mask of almost ritualized cour-
> tesy and etiquette. These rituals of deference were elaborate,
> formalized, and ever-present. They typified life in Ngelewala.

In contrast are the Hehe pastoralists (1971:96):

> One could see through the thornbush for great distances, and along
> the paths, both people and livestock seemed to exist in droves.
> Here, also unlike Ngelewala, the houses were packed together into
> nucleated settlements. But the houses were more open, with their
> thin walls, partial enclosure, and flimsy construction. Around these
> villages there were people, cattle, and much shouting and laughter.

> It was obvious that the veil of constraint and secrecy had been lifted.
> People were clearly more open, more spontaneous. They laughed
> and they quarreled openly. Everything they did was more animated.
> Women . . . chatted and giggled. . . . There was drumming, dancing,
> and singing. When men drank beer together, they talked and
> laughed loudly; and if they fought, as they frequently did, there
> were no signs of lingering acrimony.

These descriptions provide background and context for the test results.

Not surprisingly the responses to the tests vary among the four
tribes, including the farming and pastoral sections of each tribe. The
responses from each tribe, where they are different from the other tribes,
reflect a particular emphasis in values, attitudes, and emotions, a pattern of mental and emotional orientation, distinguishing one tribe from
another. Edgerton (1971:111, Table 3) shows the different responses

among the tribes for a sample question, one figure being 71 particular answers out of 123 responses for one tribe, while the other tribes gave this answer 0, 12, and 17 times out of 126, 128, and 128 answers. So the difference in response was quite marked for one tribe. Here is a brief summary of the basic elements, the particular emphasis on which characterizes that tribe, and differentiates it from the other tribes:

- Hehe: impulse aggressiveness; sensitivity to insults; self-control; sexual restraint; formal authority, and secrecy. "'We Hehe have very hot tempers and when we are fighting we cannot know what we are doing. We can even kill someone who tries to stop us'" (Edgerton 1971:111).

- Kamba: fear of poverty; male dominance; male-female antagonism; the clan; hiding emotion; affection; the land. "'The clan is the most important thing of all'" (Edgerton 1971:114).

- Pokot: cattle; physical beauty; sexual gratification; and secondarily, independence; the prophet, military bravery; depression. "'I love it. As soon as he finishes I give him food and let him sleep and then I wake him up and we do it again; we can do this all night. He works very hard to make me happy. I must have it ten times—or more'" (Edgerton 1971:116).

- Sebei: fear of death; anxiety; malignant power of women; jealousy and hostility; offspring; seniority. "'Everyone hates me—my clan, everyone'" (Edgerton 1971:119).

The tribes' different orientations could also be expressed as the tribes having different cultures. Within each tribe, the characteristic values, attitudes, and emotions expressed are learned in the individual's social context, his or her family, community, clan, tribe, and wider environment. It is noteworthy, because it indicates cultural consistency across society, that responses did not differ significantly among different age groups or between men and women, where there was largely consistent agreement (Edgerton 1971:ch. 5). The best predictor of a person's values and attitudes was his or her tribal membership. "No other consideration . . . tells us as much about a person's responses as tribal affiliation, or 'culture'" (Edgerton 1971:271). While the original research design anticipated a "controlled comparison" in which the different groups were similar if not exactly the same, the results of the study showed that the tribes' cultures were substantially different, decisively different in determining individuals' value and emotional orientations (Edgerton 1971:167). Edgerton's scrupulous methodological and analytic procedures—including multiple independent judges for coding, and an elaborate multivariate analysis to insure that simpler qualitative and quantitative analyses were not misrepresenting the data—inspire some confidence that these and subsequent findings are sound.

Edgerton's (1971: 279) other main finding is that across the four tribes, "farmers and pastoralists are differentiated on two dimensions: (1) open versus closed emotionality, and (2) direct versus indirect action." Farmers do not express their emotions freely; in fact, they go to lengths to hide their feelings.

> The farming attributes consistently relate to a central core, or theme, that might be called "interpersonal tension." For example, the farmers employ indirect action, featuring secrecy and caution; their emotions are constrained and they live with great anxiety. They not only show disrespect for authority, but the prevailing affect between people is hostility or hatred. They avoid conflict, engaging instead in litigation and witchcraft. Yet, their hostility, anxiety, and sensitivity to insults sometimes produce impulsive physical attack when open aggression does occur. (Edgerton 1971:274)

In contrast, pastoralists express their feelings freely, with little inhibition.

> Pastoralists freely express emotions, both positive emotions, such as affection, sexuality, or bravery, and dysphoric emotions such as guilt, depression, brutality, and fear of death. . . . Pastoralists act independently and aggress openly. (Edgerton 1971:276)

Characteristics that are strongly associated with pastoralism are affection, direct aggression, independence, divination, self-control, adultery, sexuality, guilt-shame, depression, and respect for authority. The differences between farmers and pastoralists are illustrated by the figure on the following page (Edgerton 1971:275, Figure 8), which summarizes characteristics and (by spatial arrangement) how distinctively they describe each group.

What explains these differences between farmers and pastoralists? The major factor is mobility: farmers are static on their land, and tied to their neighbors; pastoralists are mobile, can move from place to place with ease, and can separate from other individuals as they like.

- This means that farmers must maintain at least the appearance of cordiality, whatever their inner feelings; pastoralists can get anger off their chests, and move away if avoidance seems desirable. One finding was that the closer farmers' housing was, the stronger they felt hatred.

- Farmers must wait patiently for natural processes to bring them crops; pastoralists must assess the environmental and social situation and act to advance their goals. Divination is a procedure to draw on supernatural forces to decide what is the best course of action.

- Farmers cannot get away from the authorities over them; pastoralists can get away, and so leaders must respect public opinion among pastoralists.

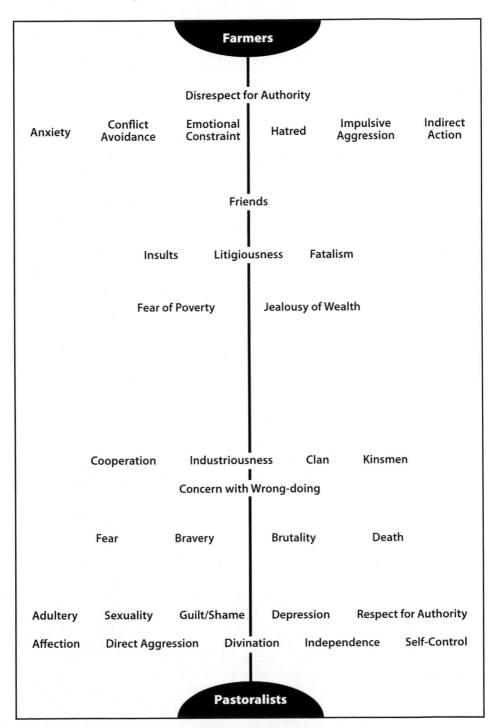

A polar comparison of farmers and pastoralists (from Edgerton 1971).

- Sexuality may reflect the greater self-expression of pastoralists.

- Guilt-shame among pastoralists reflects the need for fulfilling norms in a social context where social solidarity is useful.

- Kinsmen and clans are commonly dispersed among pastoralists, and so do not provide localized pressure but do provide a safety net; kinsmen for farmers might be near neighbors, and the cause of hatred rather than the source of help.

The African tribes that Edgerton studied not only were different from each other but were also different from tribes elsewhere. So too, African farmers and pastoralists are different from farmers and pastoralists elsewhere. However, I can attest from my own research (Salzman 2000, 2004) that many of the differences found by Edgerton in the farmers and pastoralists he studied, also distinguish farmers and pastoralists in the Middle East. The basic differences in condition in the Middle East are the same as in Africa: farmers are static and tied to their communities; pastoralists are mobile. The result is that farmers are at the mercy of their communities and rulers, while pastoralists are much more masters of their own fates. That is why farmers are dour, while pastoralists are rather more ebullient.

Chapter Four

Freedom and Equality
An Original
Illustrative Comparison

An illustrative comparison of variation among different cases, similar to those in the preceding chapter, this study originates with the author of this book and is expanded here to add material not previously published.

ARE FREEDOM AND EQUALITY COMPATIBLE?

Liberté, Égalité, Fraternité is the well-known national motto of France, deriving from the French Revolution. Leaving aside the revolutionary facts that many lost their liberty during the Terror, and others were made more equal by introduction to Professor Guillotine's efficient engine, let us inquire into the more general question of putting "liberty, equality, fraternity" into practice. Many observers, particularly in the West, would regard all three of these values as attractive and important. It is easy to find, among political philosophers and reforming politicians, advocates of one of these values over the others.

R. H. Tawney, in his book *Equality* (1952[1931]), argues that freedom is good, but only in so far as it serves equality. The view that "freedom is as freedom does" places priority on equality and/or community, as in the formula: freedom allows the rich man to eat, and the poor man to starve; the rich man to live in a palace, and the poor man to sleep under a bridge. Tawney felt that only equality would guarantee that communities have *"fraternité,"* mutual concern and solidarity. In contrast, John Stuart Mill in *On Liberty*, published in 1859 (1947:7), states that "independence is, of right, absolute. . . . The sole end for which mankind are warranted, individually or collectively, in interfering with the liberty of action of any of their number is self-protection."

Implied in these preferences is the hint that one had better choose, because it may be difficult to have all three of liberty, equality, and fraternity. Many students of this question agree. J. R. Lucas (1965, reprinted in Pojman and Westmoreland 1997:111) argues:

> Equality lays down how we are to treat people: but liberty entitles us to act as we choose, not as some rule lays down. If I have any liberty then there are some decisions I am allowed to make on my own; I am free in some cases to act arbitrarily. . . . Freedom is inherently unfair. If we place any value on Freedom at all, we must to that extent compromise the principle of Equality.

James S. Fishkin (1978, reprinted in Pojman and Westmoreland 1997:148) points out that freedom in either the private or the public sphere is incompatible with equality of results. Perhaps the most eloquent spokesman for the limitations that we face in simultaneously reaching multiple ends, is Isaiah Berlin in *Four Essays on Liberty* (1969:167–169):

> It is a commonplace that neither political equality nor efficient organization nor social justice is compatible with more than a modicum of individual liberty, and certainly not with unrestricted *laissez-faire*; that justice and generosity, public and private loyalties, the demands of genius and the claims of society, can conflict violently with each other. And it is no great way from that to the generalisation that not all good things are compatible, still less all the ideals of mankind. . . . To admit that the fufillment of some of our ideals may in principle make the fulfillment of others impossible is to say that the notion of total human fulfillment is a formal contradiction, a metaphysical chimera.

For Berlin, this is not just an "academic argument," but a critical understanding for political ideology and practical politics:

> One belief, more than any other, is responsible for the slaughter of individuals on the altars of the great historical ideals . . . the conviction that all the positive values in which men have believed must, in the end, be compatible, and perhaps even entail one another. . . . The necessity of choosing between absolute claims is then an inescapable characteristic of the human condition.

It is thus not surprising that many policy debates in Western societies—such as obligatory public vs. available private schools, obligatory trade unions vs. open shops, "progressive" vs. "equal" taxation, and public or socialized medicine vs. private medicine—turn on the relative weight to be given to freedom of the individual vs. equality of results or community uniformity. So the extent to which freedom and equality are compatible, or are inevitably alternatives about which a choice must be made, is an ongoing issue of great concern.

The political philosophers who have discussed this question tend to limit themselves to arguments, not much venturing into the world of evidence, and to be as much concerned with what should be as with what is. Social scientists, however, are mandated to pursue evidence and to base their conclusions on that. For this reason, social scientists use a variety of techniques of research, such as ethnography, or living among the people studied; surveys of material, demographic, and social factors, as well as of opinions; and examination of historical and contemporary documents. If we look across societies and cultures, drawing on evidence from these research techniques, what do we find about the relationship between freedom and equality or community? This is the question taken up by Philip Carl Salzman in "The Iron Law of Politics" (2005). Salzman ranges over a highly dispersed sample of cases to identify and discuss three basic types of society: segmentary, corporate, and market. (That discussion is augmented in the material that follows.)

SEGMENTARY SOCIETIES

In segmentary societies, of which a number will be referenced here, each group or unit—lineage or village, clan, tribal section, tribe, tribal confederation—is much like the next; that is, there is no specialist differentiation of function, and no division of labor between groups. Segmentary societies are tribal societies or independent or quasi-independent village societies.

In tribal segmentary societies, raiding and warfare are endemic, and violence a way of life. The need for security and the quest for power, wealth, and reputation generate a constant bellicose struggle. As William Lancaster reports in *The Rwala Bedouin* (1997[1981]), Emir Nuri Sha'alan of the Rwala Bedouin produced, through a long series of multiple marriages, 39 sons. Of these, 37 died violently, mostly in raids, seeking fame and fortune before they married, and the 38th was killed after he married but before he had children. "The [camel] economy was booming, the inner desert was still inviolate and raiding and warfare extremely bloody" (Lancaster 1997[1981]:137).

As well as among the Bedouin, we see this clearly with the Nuer raiding Dinka villages, stealing cattle, burning huts, killing the "useless" elderly, and expanding into the "cleansed" territory; the Yomut Turkmen and the Sarhadi Baluch raiding Persian villages for slaves, livestock, and carpets, and raiding caravans for merchandise; and, in the meanwhile, the Nuer, Turkmen, and Baluch fighting among themselves, both within and between tribes, over threats or injuries or to profit from opportunities.

And no less do the mountain-dwelling Kurds, Pakhtuns, and Berbers rely upon force of arms to secure their land and livestock, their property and persons, and to bring in new resources and open up other land to their use. Barth (1953:116) described the Hamawand Kurds as "adapting their whole society to an economy based on war and looting." Lindholm (2002:86 and passim) has described the "continuous and fruitless struggles for power" characteristic of segmentary tribal societies, although he acknowledges that from time to time tribes, as Ibn Khaldun—an Arab official and scholar, born in North Africa in 1332— theorizes, succeed in conquering and ruling settled societies.

In segmentary societies, every man, barring a few ritual specialists, is a warrior. In addition to knowing how to herd or farm, every man has to know how to fight. And every man expects to engage in combat from time to time, at the very least, but has to be vigilant at all times and ready to fight at any moment. In the early Arab Empire, with a population made up largely of Bedouin, "the citizen list was the army register, the tribes and families forming the regiments and companies" (quoted in Lindholm 2002:85–86). The population and the army coincided! And off to raid and fight they went, with great effect, bringing the Arab Empire conquest upon conquest, occupying and ruling region after region. When that ended, they once again took up fighting amongst themselves.

Even in agrarian societies, such as in 19th-century Italy, in the space not effectively controlled by state coercion, local populations, such as highland Sardinians and rural Sicilians, operated independently using self-help to advance their security and interests. In contrast to tribal segmentary self-help, peasant segmentary self-help was characterized by nuclear family segments rather than larger lineages—individuals acting secretly, rather than groups acting in the open, rustling and destroying property rather than raiding and looting, vendetta rather than warfare. Sardinian shepherds in highland pastures and Sicilian rural "managers" relied upon violence to protect their property and reputations and to advance their interests and control. In defense, others did likewise. Attacks, shootings, burnings, bombings, and assassinations were common, and only those successful at intimidation had any hope of peace, precarious though it was.

In a world with security provided by segmentary self-help, life might not have been solitary, and perhaps not brutish, but it *was* brutal and beset with, in Thomas Hobbes' words, "continual fear, and danger of violent death." Peace and security might have been hoped for but were not expected. A reliable civil peace in which disputes would be resolved without resort to violence was unheard of, almost beyond imagination.

But while lacking in peace and security, segmentary self-help has other qualities—beyond the exhilarating exercise of violence and uplifting challenge to be heroic—that have proven widely attractive. These qualities are freedom, or individual autonomy, and equality. Let us look at a case that illustrates individual autonomy.

Lancaster (1997[1981]:67) reports that, among the Rwala Bedouin, "direct teaching stops when a child is five or six. After that he (or she) learns from direct experience that he is on his own and is, from now on, directly responsible for his own actions and future." For example:

> An eight-year-old boy is expected to avenge the killing of his father—if the opportunity offers and there is no one else available he must, for family honour is at stake. This is by no means only theoretical. The eight-year-old son of the Emir of the Rwala, armed with a penknife and helped by a few friends his own age, attempted to storm the central prison in Damascus to secure the release of his uncle. No one thought his action comic or stupid—it was generally regarded as absolutely correct and laudable, if somewhat misguided. (Lancaster 1997[1981]:67–68)

Similarly, regarding the decision to attend school or not, "personal autonomy is so highly prized that such decisions are made by the child, although parents will advise" (Lancaster 1997[1981]:103). Lancaster (1997[1981]:136) characterizes Rwala society as "one where every man is equally free to follow his own bent" and "every man is an island and is responsible for his own affairs." In all areas of life—including with whom one associates, where one lives or travels, how one makes a living, how one allocates one's resources, and with whom one fights—decisions are up to the individual, for "no man has power over another," no man rules, and none is a subject:

> No individual has political power, no group has political power and no family has political power; power is restricted to the workings of public opinion. Even public opinion has no formal coercive power; co-operation can be withdrawn and that is all. All men are autonomous and equal and there is no mechanism whereby these principles can be overridden. The Bedu system is based on the premises of equality, autonomy and the acquisition of reputation. (Lancaster 1997[1981]:77)

Material resources did not count for much in themselves. The Rwala depended upon camels for food and transport, but no family needed more than 20. Wealth among the Rwala was reckoned not in material holdings but in reputation, which came from success in raiding for camels and generosity in donating camels to others. As Lancaster (1997[1981]:140) puts it, "raiding converts camels into reputation." Rwala differed as to reputation and thus prestige, but in political status and in accumulated material wealth no divisions were established, no great differences of position, no hierarchies or stratification.

Security based on self-help, an inviolable individual autonomy, and a determined insistence on equality were general throughout the tribal Middle East, as Lindholm, in *The Islamic Middle East*, (2002:20, 24) testifies:

> The conditions of the desert correlate with the deep-seated resistance of camel nomads to hierarchy and stratification. . . . [Among the large, sheep-herding confederacies of western Iran,] despite the khans' objective authority, the nomads retained strongly egalitarian ideologies, and did not accept their leaders as intrinsically superior to them. The arbitrary power of leaders in these shepherd communities was therefore sharply limited by their well-founded fear of their fellow tribesmen, who might decide to eliminate, or at least abandon, an overly-ambitious or oppressive "authority."

Similarly, among mountain tribesmen "the faith in human equality and the pursuit of personal honor are the essence of the proper way of being" (Lindholm 2002:25–26). These tribesmen commonly make an invidious distinction between their own land as *yaghestan* or *siba,* the land of freedom, and *hukomat* or *makhzen,* the despised land of governance where oppressed peasants are enslaved by taxation. Lindholm sums up: "Middle Eastern peripheral peoples—camel nomads, shepherds, and mountain farmers—unanimously maintain ideologies of egalitarianism and personal independence." This is confirmed by accounts of other Middle Eastern tribal peoples, such as the Cyrenaican Bedouin, the Al Murrah Bedouin, Yomut Turkmen, Harasiis Bedouin, and Sarhadi Baluch.

The pattern described for Middle Eastern tribal peoples is equally evident among African peoples. Among the Somali, that "fierce and turbulent race of Republicans," as Richard Burton (quoted in Lewis, *A Pastoral Democracy* 1961:v) described them in the 19th century, both individual liberty and equality are presumptions and operating principles. Lewis (1961:1) refers to the Somalis' "extreme independence and individualism," and to each Somali's "firm conviction that he is sole master of his actions and subject to no authority except that of God." The Somali political system has traditionally been based on "an egalitarian social contract," thus categorizing Somali society as a member of "that class of egalitarian societies with little social stratification and no centralized government." Lewis (1961:196) elaborates:

> In principle, all adult males have an equal say, since all can speak in the councils of their group. Naturally, however, the opinions of different men carry different weight. Here status differences refer to wealth, inherited prestige, skill in public oratory and poetry, political acumen, age, wisdom, and other personal characteristics.

Significant differences can arise in wealth as embodied in livestock or as derived from trade. Accordingly, "Somali are well aware of the power which wealth brings, and at the same time, of the responsibilities which it entails in the support of poorer kinsmen" (Lewis 1961:197). These "poorer kinsmen," along with political supporters outside the kin structure, thus become beneficiaries of excess and, in return, clients of the wealthy.

The distribution of livestock wealth is widespread in pastoral tribal societies. Among many, such as the Karimojong, it is well institutionalized, as Dyson-Hudson in *Karimojong Politics* (1966:84, 91) relates:

> A man will give as many cattle as he reasonably can in bridewealth. This form of wealth dispersal is considered an eminently suitable use for cattle assets. It provides the groom with as extensive an affinal kin group as he can afford. By the wide dispersal of bridewealth shares, it provides him also with a greatly increased range of "cattle kin" who are his mainstay in trouble of all kinds. It is cattle kin, as a group, that provide any man with his most reliable supporters, since quarrels of any kind are likely to involve payment or receipt or at least well-being of cattle, and in terms of cattle the interest of one member is substantially the interest of them all.

The picture among the Nuer appears to be similar. Evans-Pritchard, in *The Nuer* (1940:20, 91, 296) stresses the ongoing process of redistribution of livestock, the main form of their wealth:

> There is little inequality of wealth and no class privilege. It is true that cattle can be amassed, but in fact they are not. . . . When a herd has reached a certain size the owner—if one may speak of an owner of a herd in which many people have rights of one kind and another—is morally bound to dispose of a portion of it by either himself marrying or by assisting a relative to do so. . . . [The result is that] cattle are everywhere evenly distributed. Hardly any one is entirely without them, and no one is very rich. Although cattle are a form of wealth that can be accumulated, a man never possesses many more beasts than his byre will hold, because as soon as his herd is large enough he, or one of his family, marries. Every household goes through these alternating periods of poverty and comparative wealth. Marriages and epidemics prevent accumulation of cattle and [thus] no disparity in wealth offends the democratic sentiment of the people.

> Among the Nuer, equality is no inhibition to autonomy and freedom, the Nuer constitution [being] highly individualistic and libertarian.

> The ordered anarchy in which they live accords well with their character, for it is impossible to live among Nuer and conceive of rulers ruling over them.

> The Nuer is a product of hard and egalitarian upbringing, is deeply democratic, and is easily roused to violence. His turbulent spirit finds any restraint irksome and no man recognizes a superior.

> That every Nuer considers himself as good as his neighbour is evi-
> dent in their every movement. They strut about like lords of the
> earth, which, indeed, they consider themselves to be. There is no
> master and no servant in their society, but only equals who regard
> themselves as God's noblest creation. [A Nuer] does not consider
> himself bound to obey any one.

And any vision of Nuer as social or spatial prisoner to the structural dictates of the lineage system is definitively contradicted by
Evans-Pritchard's (1940:210; see also Evans-Pritchard 1951:28) reports
of voluntaristic moving and mixing as Nuer pursue their preferred individual destinies:

> Nuer have always felt themselves free to wander as they pleased,
> and if a man is unhappy, his family sick, his herds declining, his
> garden exhausted, his relations with some of his neighbours uncon-
> genial, or merely if he is restless, he moves to a different part of the
> country and resides with some kinsmen.

In segmentary societies, in spite of insecurity and danger, free and
autonomous men, and, to a degree, women, share their wealth, creating
egalitarian societies with, to a substantial degree, an equal distribution
of wealth. How is this to be understood? The answer is clear: free individuals share their wealth not "in spite of insecurity and danger" but
because of insecurity and danger. Wealth is allocated to others as a way
of building cohesion for security. As I. M. Lewis (1976:176) astutely put it:

> The more one produces the more one is expected to give away; the
> positive side of the equation is that the greater one's generosity the
> stronger and more comprehensive one's corresponding entitlement
> to support and succour in time of need. [People freely redistribute
> and share their surplus wealth because they do so on] this very ra-
> tional basis of enlightened self-interest. Material wealth is trans-
> formed into social assets.

Security is thus enhanced in the only way it can be in a segmentary society: through the active support of other people. Because fellow
group members share a common interest in security, and because security is counted in the number of allies, people are willing to distribute
their material resources, thus advancing economic equality. This is
why, in segmentary societies, liberty and equality are found together.
The institution that motivates people to share freely is self-help, security through group action. But at the same time, what is absent in segmentary societies, is civil peace based on rules and enforced by peace
and security agents. The opportunity cost for members of segmentary
societies, in which much attention, time, and effort by all members is
devoted to security, is that much talent and effort is unavailable for economic and cultural development. So while segmentary societies can
enjoy both freedom and equality, they do so at a great cost.

CORPORATE SOCIETIES

Peasant Corporate Societies:
The Case of Highland Sardinia

If in the remote communal pastures of highland Sardinia a war of every shepherd against every shepherd persists, then just as surely in the island's permanent highland villages and agrotowns, graced with stone houses and orchards and home to shepherds' families and from time to time shepherds themselves, a deeply established *contrasting* sentiment persists: not "all for one and one for all," typically a tribal ideology, but "all for a sense of oneness, and each one had better act appropriately" (Salzman 1999a:ch. 3). For the Italian *comune*, the territory with its centralized settlement and *frazioni* (other small settlements), is, like the Spanish *pueblo* (Pitt-Rivers 1961[1954]), a community of orientation, of ongoing reference and primary loyalty, as well as, presently, an official municipality, a local level of governmental organization. These local Mediterranean communities have tended to be inner-looking, seeking employment from community resources and holding to endogamy. The unity of the community and the corresponding sense of belonging are much valued by residents. And residents' actions are assessed, to substantial degree, as contributions to that unity.

Equality is prized, in these Sardinian *comuni*, as a reflection of unity and solidarity. No one is better or worse than anyone else; everyone is the same: a member of the community. Inequality is feared as a threat to solidarity and unity, in that it might divide the community, highlighting how members differ from one another rather than what they have in common: their community membership. Thus behaviors that make people stand out, or remarkable successes, draw serious disapproval. Even staying at home and not mixing with others in the street or in the bar is regarded as a serious violation of community solidarity. Differences in style of dress, in music, in occupational or intellectual interests—all result in negative comments and a degree of ostracism. Some residents have left, or plan to leave, because of what they regard as the oppressive atmosphere in their town. But others, of course, relish their established place in the community, their sense of belonging and solidarity among community members.

Material success beyond that of others is a major threat, felt to undermine community. The response to such success is *invidia*, envy, and leads to attempts to reestablish community equilibrium by bringing successful individuals back to a "normal level." This is done through violent attacks—by fire, bombs, firearms—on the material sources and symbols of his or her superiority, as well as on his or her reputation and standing by the spreading of rumors and the fabrication of scandal. For example, in 1993 a recently built factory, one of the few in Villagrande Strisaili, a highland agrotown in the central Sardinian region of Ogliastra, was bombed and largely destroyed by unknown hands. No competitors operated either locally or regionally, so the bombing was not thought to have been an intra-industry crime. Nor had any attempts at extortion for "protection" preceded the event; Sardinia has no established mafia. Local opinion indicated that invidia was behind the bombing. This explanation gained credibility in light of a high frequency of *attentati*, attacks, on successful local entrepreneurs. The general view expressed was that Villagrandesi were delighted when one of their number gained success away, on the coast or in the city, but were not willing to tolerate one of them doing exceptionally well at home in Villagrande.

In these closed, corporate communities of highland Sardinia, equality and identity form the ideal, and freedom is seen as a threat to that ideal. Acting unconventionally, marrying out of the community, leaving to live elsewhere, succeeding economically to an egregious degree, and gaining political office are all seen as violations of solidarity and threats to unity. According to community norms, individual freedom must be sacrificed for the collectivity, for which economic equality is required. Economic equality and individual freedom are at odds. In the past, individual freedom has been sacrificed for equality. To the extent that recently greater individual freedom has been able to assert itself in the face of the violent resistance generated by invidia, the equality and identity of community members and the unity of the community have suffered. Highland Sardinians are presently struggling to find a balance—between increased freedom and decreased equality—with which they can live.

This emphasis on solidarity and unity is typical of corporate communities. A well known example is the "corporate' village of highland Latin America, so labeled and described in Eric Wolf's 1955 paper, "Types of Latin American Peasantry" (summarized in ch. 3, above).

Among philosophers, too, the desirability of solidarity and unity in a collectivity is a major rationale justifying equality. Tawney in *Equality* (1952:111–112) argued that "a high degree of practical [economic and material] equality is necessary because a community requires unity." After all, he (1952:118) continued, "social well-being depends upon cohesion and solidarity, a strong sense of common interests, and a common enterprise which is the concern of all." Underlying was Tawney's belief in "the fact of human fellowship, which is ultimate and profound, [and which] should [not] be obscured by economic contrasts, which are trivial and superficial."

Equality in aid of the common interest and unity of the collectivity, or fraternity, was realized, according to Tawney (1952:103), in the soviet communist societies of eastern Europe: "The last chapter of the story [of liberation from economic and political oppression] which was begun in 1789 has been written in eastern Europe since 1918." For our purposes, these former soviet countries provide examples of complex societies, substantially urbanized and industrialized, organized on the corporate model. The means of production and capital resources generally, such as land, factories, stores, and housing, were nationalized and owned by society as a whole. Economies were centrally planned and commanded. States, purportedly on behalf of their peoples, controlled production and allocation of products; goods and services were intended to be distributed widely and evenly—that is, fairly and equitably. Everyone was supposed to receive all necessities for a secure life.

Did soviet societies deliver economic equality? To a degree they did; basic goods and services were distributed widely, however questionable their quantity and quality. There was no class of rich property owners. But not all citizens had equal access to state resources; state villas, limousines, and personal services were under the control of state officials, and they had use of them "on behalf of the people." So while no significant differentiation was allowed in terms of ownership, substantial differentiation existed in terms of use rights. Still, all considered, the soviet societies did achieve a qualified success in the establishment of economic equality.

But the soviet societies were anything but bastions of individual freedom. The "dictatorship of the proletariat" turned out to be dictatorship by the state apparatus. Political opposition was regarded as worse than illegitimate; it was treated as a sign of insanity and was often rewarded by a one-way ticket to a "mental hospital." Suspect groups were transported to marginal regions, imprisoned in "work camps," starved, or directly executed. Even for those regarded as good citizens, travel and access to information were severely restricted. Jobs and housing were allocated by state functionaries. Choice and availability of services and products were greatly limited. In short, safeguards against state interference and safeguards *for* freedoms of speech, of association, of movement, and of choice were largely absent, and so personal liberty was nugatory.

Corporate Societies: The Case of Cuba

These general assertions about communist societies can be illustrated with the case of Cuba. After the conquest of the Batista regime by Fidel Castro in 1958, Cuba was shaped by a vision, a Revolutionary vision defined by Castro's ideals. "The Cuban Communist Party attempted to instill Revolutionary values in the populace and to forge citizens' behaviours as a means of achieving the ideals envisioned by Castro" (Bertrand 2009:16).

In order for the Cuban people to be free of exploitation, and to be raised from poverty, Cuba had to be free from US domination and from internal exploiters. Castro engaged in a number of basic legal and economic reforms to bring this about: agricultural land reform; new urban housing and rent control; full employment; and free education and health care (Bertrand 2009: 18–19). But more than this: Castro set out "not to control the country, but to empower the masses" (Bertrand 2009:19).

Empowerment of the population was to be brought about by political education, which would generate a Revolutionary national consciousness. For their part, the Cuban people were expected to conform to the model of the *Hombre Nuevo*, New Man. According to Che Guevara, the New Man "expressed in both his thoughts and actions the values of nationalism, self-sacrifice for the greater good of society, egalitarianism, communalism, and loyalty to the nation, the Cuban people, socialism, and Castro" (Bertrand 2009:20). "The educational program and the mass media served as socialization tools to infuse the populace with values intimately linked with Castro's vision of an ideal Cuba" (Bertrand 2009:19).

Castro emphasized uprightness and incorruptibility, arguing that "an ideal man always chooses civic duty over better standards of living" (Bertrand 2009:21). The New Man was devoted to the Revolution, conformed to its values, and pursued its goals relentlessly. Castro's vision was unitary and encompassing: "'Within the Revolution everything, against the Revolution nothing'" (Bertrand 2009:21). It was also oppositional and agonistic: Revolutionary Cuba was in an ongoing struggle against its arch enemy, the United States and its Cuban exiles. But not only against the enemy, also against their capitalist system that encouraged selfish individualism at the expense of other individuals and the collectivity. The Cuban ideal was selflessness in support of the collectivity and the Revolution, and noncompetitive conformity to Revolutionary ideals (Bertrand 2009:21–22).

The standards of Revolutionary morality were narrow and strict. Behavior was assessed by the standards. "Exhibiting non-Revolutionary values is therefore seen as antisocial behavior and as a hindrance to the success of Revolutionary ideals" (Bertrand 2009:22). Non-Revolutionary behavior came to be seen as anti-Revolutionary behavior. It was but a small step to the criminalization of behavior that did not conform to Revolutionary ideals.

To guarantee the success of the Revolution, it was necessary to mobilize the population in favor of it, and to establish mechanisms of control to ensure correct behavior and punish incorrect behavior. According to José Ramón Ponce Solozábal (2006:91), sometime Cuban counterintelligence psychological specialist and professor of applied psychology at the National Counterintelligence School of Cuba:

> Countries like Cuba are clearing houses for socio-psychological techniques that aim at achieving the major objectives of all totali-

tarian regimes: absolute political power by asserting total control over every aspect of a population's social, political, economic, and moral life.

These techniques, including those of communication and propaganda, "have as their objective channeling and modifying existing mores, beliefs, feelings, motivations, and emotions in a manner that leads to cultural and psychological submission to the state" (Ponce Solozábal 2006:92). He (2006:95) specifies further:

> Choice is closely circumscribed across a spectrum of activities, including what is acceptable for a person to hear in the news or to buy in a store, where a person can live, what he can do for a living, and where he can travel. Compliance with such measures is promoted as a necessary patriotic duty and is subject to state monitoring.

It is quite clear from this description that what is absent in virtually all spheres for Cubans is freedom, and that state action is aimed precisely at curtailing freedom. Let us now explore briefly the mechanisms by which this is done.

A central strategy for controlling the population is influencing its attitudes. How does the Castro regime go about shaping the views of its subjects? Ponce Solozábal (2006:93–94, emphasis added) argues:

> The Cuban regime imposes a mental and spiritual yoke upon the population. It conditions the psychological outlook of the populace through a calculated policy that narrows expectations by *limiting individual choices across the social spectrum.* . . . Castro's regime has gradually habituated the Cuban population to accept, in large part unconsciously, *a social, political and economic environment in which lack of choice is the norm.* Therefore, a life of limited choice that produces accepted dependence on the state has become the virtual psychology status quo; it is an element now entrenched in the national character of the Cuban population itself.

Some of the themes that the regime strives to inculcate in the population include (1) the infallibility and omnipotence of the regime, and thus the impossibility of opposing it; (2) the right of the state—which is alleged to represent the interests of the people—to "absolute control of property" and "strict regulation of individual liberties" (Ponce Solozábal 2006:94); (3) the right of the state, and its agencies the police and secret service, to monitor and control the behavior and activities of the population; (4) the reliability and truth of the state-controlled media and the information stemming from that source; and (5) the benefit of the state's absolute control of movement, both internally and externally, of the population.

Charismatic leadership is a great aid to imposing total control over a population. A personality cult of the leader gives image and strength to the regime. The leader becomes the personification of the regime, becomes himself a focus of loyalty. We have seen this in the China of Mao, in North Korea with Kim Jong-il, and, of course, in Cuba with Fidel Castro (Ponce Solozábal 2006). For a personality cult to be effective, the leader must address, if not in fact satisfy, the needs and desires of the population. The other side of the coin is mass demonstrations that whip up feelings of unity, solidarity, support of the regime, and anger toward its alleged enemies (Ponce Solozábal 2006:97–98).

The most efficient and effective way to support the regime is to convince Cubans that it is the font of all virtue and security. In other words, if Cubans internalize, in their minds, the views of the regime, then support follows automatically. How does it do this? According to the sociologist B. E. Aguirre (2000:4):

> Its government has been in uninterrupted power for close to 40 years, long enough to create institutions, collective memories and facts as part of a more or less cogent national cultural policy. It has total command of formal education and the mass media. It has a near monopoly of the information and interpretations used by Cubans to make sense of their social world. The government is assiduously attentive to the provision of explanations and creation and enforcement of norms shaping people's beliefs regarding the exercise of political power, explanations which become "officially-imagined worlds" providing political legitimacy to the government.

Shaping the thoughts of its subjects is thus a primary focus of the Revolutionary regime. The education system is a basic tool in this quest (Aguirre 2000:8):

> The institution of education forms part of the natural, taken-for-granted world of Cuban people, which, repeated in many different institutional and substantive contexts, constitutes the primary source of support of the ideology of domination of the government and the political stability of the regime.

In other words, schools teach the ideas, ideals, views, values, prescriptions, and proscriptions of the regime. Alternative views outside of the government framework are given no hearing. Freedom of thought and intellectual exploration are not only discouraged, but are condemned as immoral.

Further in its defense, the regime sets up control institutions that permeate the entire society and touch all members of the population. These include the Revolutionary Defense Committees, the Federation of Cuban Women, Communist Party trade unions, the University Students Federation, the High School Students Federation, etc. These organizations fill a number of important functions: monitor general opinion and individual attitudes and behavior; apply pressure for conformity; provide a controlled outlet for disaffection; diffuse rumors supportive of the regime and deleterious to any opposition; identify potential leaders;

allow rapid mobilization, as for demonstrations (Ponce Solozábal 2006: 99; Aguirre 2000:9). From the point of view of the individual, belonging to these organizations sponsored by the state is the main, and often the only, means of social and economic mobility. To be a militant—active in the Communist youth, or in a trade union, or in the student federation—opens occupational and consumption possibilities that are closed to nonmembers. The Revolution takes care of its own!

All of these organizations are overseen by government security agencies, of which there are several. Central of course is the Ministry of the Interior (MININT). Among its departments are the *Departamento Tecnico de Investigaciones* (DTI), the National Revolutionary Police (PNR), and the *Departamento de Seguiridad del Estado* (DSE), Department of State Security (Aguirre 2000:10). Each of these departments has units and agents operating throughout the country and in all labor, educational, and other organizations. These departments, especially the DSE, which focuses on political "crimes," is constantly on the watch for "incorrect" behavior. In every organization, in every meeting, the presence of security agents, "whether real or assumed, overt or covert, informs the behavior of participants in these gatherings" (Aguirre 2000:8).

Let us examine in a bit more detail one of these organizations, the *Comités de Defensa de la Revoluceón,* the Committees for the Defense of the Revolution. One of its arms is the *Vigilancia y Orden Público,* Vigilance and Public Order (VOP). At the lowest level of the VOP is an agent in charge of several neighborhood blocks of dwellings or buildings, who must keep a file on each resident and a daily log of all activities (Ragolta 1983:1). A special unit of the VOP is the Prevention and Education Front, which focuses on young people who are not in school and do not have jobs. The VOP works directly with the uniformed police and reports all relevant information to them, as well as reporting up the VOP hierarchy. (A parallel structure in the Ministry of the Interior places another agent in each block, who reports directly to an officer of the security apparatus of the Ministry.) The VOP recruits people loyal to the regime who will make every effort to uncover any wrongdoing on the part of the populace. Reports of wrongdoing will lead to intervention by a sector controller of the VOP, who will give warnings. The third intervention leads to the arrest of the accused (Ragolta 1983:2).

In an appendix attached to the reprinted Ragolta article, there is a report from Pax Christi Netherlands (PCN), based on a visit to Cuba in 1995. PCN describes the Committees for the Defense of the Revolution as follows:

> CDR members spy on their neighbors and, in turn, urge them to spy on others and fill out "Opinion Collection Forms" about what they hear their neighbors and colleagues saying during the course of daily

life, particularly their political opinions. The completed forms are then passed on by the CDRs to the police and MININT [Ministry of the Interior]. The CDRs also rely on networks of *chivatos*, "stool pigeons," to gather information on people's behavior. . . .

Fear is the basic instrument of political control. The information at the State Security's disposal can be used to threaten and intimidate anybody, including those who oppose the regime, to force them to go along with the established ideology. . . . There is no place to escape the tentacles of the State. The distrust is unbearable.

The PCN estimate is that there are 80,000 members of the CDR, in a population of around 11 million; thus there is one CDR member for every 140 Cubans.

Ragolta (1983:3), a sometime functionary of the Cuban Government, is at pains to point out how different the CDR VOP, the *Brigadas de Respuesta Rápida* (Rapid Response Brigades), and other Cuban mass organizations are from "civil society":

The notion of civil society is alien to the policies that the Cuban leadership is pursuing at present. The theories of "transmission belts" and an "enlightened vanguard" suit more closely [the] regime's goals and modus operandi. The essence of civil society lies in the possibility that social groups could be autonomous, particularly from military and government tutelage and control. This is impossible in today's Cuban society.

Ragolta (1983:3) concludes by arguing that "The revolutionary leadership and the leader himself have designed a totalitarian society."

However, Cuba and the Castro regime do not live only in their constructed society, but also in history. Things happen outside the reach and control of the Castro regime, things that drastically change the conditions under which the regime must operate. There could hardly be a more dramatic example than the fall in 1991 of the Soviet Union, Cuba's ally, supporter, and subsidizer. Without Soviet aid, without Soviet purchases of Cuban goods at inflated prices, Cuba faced penury and bankruptcy. Radical measures were necessary to generate new income. The strategy devised by the regime was a shift from primary production to service, from export to import: the development of tourist facilities on this tropical island, especially on the coasts and beaches, to attract well-to-do tourists with hard currency, all of course under the control of the State. Tourists developments are joint ventures between foreign investors and the State. The State supplies service employees of their choice, and pays them in Cuban currency; employees receive hard currency only in tips. As a result of this shift of orientation, a redefinition of revolutionary identity and morality has taken place: "revolutionary behaviour is now equated to bringing prestige and money to Cuba" (Bertrand 2009:23). And the main venue is the new and rapidly developing tourist sector.

The decline of primary production and of the internal Cuban economy, combined with the focus on the tourist sector and the attraction of external wealth, has resulted in a division of the economy between the internal and external economies. Those who work for government enterprises—sugar farmers, teachers, doctors, etc.—and this includes most Cubans, have seen the real value of their income decline and with it their ability to pay for the most basic necessities of life. In contrast, those who work in the tourist sector and provide services to tourists are able to gain valuable hard currency and can shop in Cuban hard currency shops for commodities not even available for Cubans with Cuban currency. This new economic orientation of the government, called the "Special Period," and its consequences for the population, have led to considerable disillusion among the people. In the past, the government was committed to socialism and to taking care of people's needs; now, the government is more concerned with making money and no longer takes care of people's needs. During the 1980s, before the fall of the Soviet Union, the government was looking out for the population, and people felt reasonably well-off, or at least it seems that way in retrospect. Now, people dependent on the internal economy feel abandoned by the government, a government that appears to have abandoned socialism.

From these developments have arisen a new modus operandi among Cubans dependent on the internal economy. They have sought new means to satisfy their basic survival needs. These new means are outside of the accepted procedures of the Cuban economy and have generated among the Cuban population a parallel culture of illegality (Bertrand 2009:24). Many Cubans feel that as the government has strayed from socialism and its obligations to support the people, and has encouraged a new inequality of wealth, the Cuban Revolutionary norms of socialist activity, and their prohibition of bourgeois activities, are no longer binding. "Cubans have noticed that individualist and capitalist behaviours bring more rewards today than exhibiting Revolutionary fervour and morality" (Bertrand 2009:28). In any case, people must live, and find ways to fill their basic needs.

The circumstances of Cubans dependent on the internal economy have deteriorated since the initiation of the Special Period in the following ways (Bertrand 2009:28-31): First, the official food supply has declined. There are fewer items on the rationed goods list, and even they are not always available at the peso stores. In contrast there are many more goods available in dollar stores, but most Cubans do not have dollars. Housing for Cubans is dilapidated and declining, but collapsed or unoccupied buildings are being sold to foreign enterprises for use as tourist hotels or stores. Third, the guaranteed employment of the past has disappeared, as the government lays off agricultural workers, paying them a small pension. Fourth, health and education sectors have declined at least in part because the professional staff are so

poorly paid that they reduce their input or abandon the work altogether in search of better opportunities in the tourism sector. Standards for hiring teachers have been reduced to fill the slots. The
government sends Cuban doctors abroad, such as to Venezuela, leaving
fewer and less distinguished doctors at home. As well, money for dollar
stores or for bribes for hospital staff are necessary to receive needed
medicine and treatment.

In these circumstances, what do Cubans do? Food is bought on the
black market. Jobs are found in black market activities. Friends and
relatives are turned to for housing. Bribes are paid when resources
allow. In short, Cubans can no longer rely on the government to satisfy
their basic needs, and have had to rely on their own initiatives. Of
course, this goes against government ideology, which demands that
Cubans contribute to the collectivity rather than seek to satisfy their
individual needs and interests. But as the government has in practice
defaulted on its commitments, Cubans regard government ideological
demands as null and void. The failures of the government to fulfill its
commitments to provide the basic necessities for all Cubans, are exacerbated by the blatant inequality generated by the government-sponsored division of peso and dollar sectors. This has undermined any
government claim on the basis of socialist ideology. Furthermore, there
is an enforced segregation of ordinary Cubans, aside from those in the
tourist service sector, from foreigners, reducing travel and access to
facilities for ordinary Cubans. And the necessity to offer the best quality Cuban goods to tourists has reduced the quality of goods available
to ordinary Cubans. So the legitimacy of the government has fallen in
the eyes of the population, and Revolutionary ideals have become moot
in the face of daily circumstances (Bertrand 2009:28–36).

Ordinary Cubans do not see their deviance from Revolutionary
ideals as rebellion or even resistance. Rather, they think of it as coping.
They apply two concepts to their parallel culture of illegality: The first
is *inventar*, literally "to invent," which refers to people finding solutions
through their imagination and creativity. The second is *resolver*, literally "to take care of something" or "solve a problem," meaning to use
one's position and relationships to gain access to scarce goods and services. "Together, these concepts testify to the emergence of a parallel
culture characterized by a widespread involvement in illegality and the
complex networks necessary to sustain it" (Bertrand 2009:46).

The Special Period and its new focus on tourism and the hard currency it brings has not seen a decline in State control of the Cuban population. According to Aguirre (2000:12), "the most important post-1989
change in the system of state repression is the comparatively greater
importance given to reactive rather than proactive approaches to social
control." The government will crack down on black market activities
whenever it sees fit. To take just one example, some Cubans make

black market Havana cigars, outside of authorized government factories. They make a living at this, but their position is less than secure:

> "I'm always scared," said Pedro as he deftly twisted large tobacco leaves to make fake famous-name Havana cigars in a clandestine workshop in the Cuban capital. If caught in his illegal workshop, known as a *"chinchal,"* Pedro would face a prison term. (Zygel 2009:FW3)

In some other activities, such as internal travel and access to services, Cubans are more restricted by government measures than previously. Furthermore, the government allocated the favored new jobs in the tourist sector only to its favorites, that is, those who strongly support, or purport to strongly support, the regime. There is perhaps more tolerance in practice on the part of government agents as regards minor illegalities on the part of Cubans as they seek to take care of themselves. But public policy remains totally in the hands of the regime, with no chance of correction by the populace. Resistance to the regime, threats to the regime, even peaceful ones, are not tolerated, and are often violently crushed (Aguirre 2000:10–14). The structures of control remain, and remain vigilant. The Cuban Government remains a regime that demands conformity and unity, and forbids freedom of thought and action.

In corporate societies, economic equality is instituted to serve the basic needs of all members of the community, and to advance the solidarity of community members and thus the unity of the community. Any individual actions that would threaten that equality and unity have to be excluded, and thus individual liberty is greatly restricted where not entirely precluded. Civil peace is present, in both peasant and soviet corporate societies, instituted by the community as a collectivity or by the state. In sum, in corporate society, both economic equality and civil peace are to a substantial degree present, while individual freedom is largely absent.

MARKET SOCIETIES AND LIBERAL DEMOCRACIES

Market societies, such as the open peasant societies of Latin America described by Wolf (1955), do away with the group-imposed restrictions of closed corporate societies and give much greater freedom to individual families and individuals. In economic activity, people are tied to the market and must adapt to market fluctuations. Among families, there is considerable economic inequality; for particular families and individuals, market fluctuations mean variation over time in income. So too in industrial, capitalist societies, where families and individuals have greatly variant economic positions, even considering upward and downward mobility. At the same time, families and individuals have great freedom in pursuing education, in choosing occupations, in making investments and expenditures, as well as in a wide range of civil liberties. Here great liberty is wedded with great economic inequality.

Capitalist liberal democracies, a subcategory of market societies distinct from despotic market societies such as China in the 21st century, draw on traditions that assert the value of both freedom and equality. The motto of the French Revolution, "Liberty, Equality, Fraternity," is one such source. The abrupt French rejection of hereditary power in favor of "liberty and equality" was followed by a gradual series of reforms in Great Britain to the same effect. The primacy of these values and goals is unquestioned today in liberal democracies and is invoked frequently. For example, in a recent commentary, Kennedy (2009:A11) has asserted that "Canada is founded on a core belief in equality, actual and perceived. The people who shaped this nation did so from a premise . . . and principles that cherish personal freedom. For all."

"Freedom" and "equality" are the touchstones of liberal democratic political culture. The significance of many substantive issues rests with how freedom or equality are advanced or curtailed. True, these are not the only references; "prosperity," "order," and "peace" are also important. And of course the very meanings of "freedom" and "equality" are contested. For example, it is common today in liberal democracies of Europe and North America for "multiculturalism" to be an established value. Multiculturalism, and its associated principles of "diversity" and "tolerance," is justified by reference to "equality," with regard to the asserted equality of collectivities: ethnic or cultural groups. Whatever one's argument in contemporary liberal democracies, one must find a way to invoke "equality" on its behalf.

However, liberal democrats face a dilemma because their ideals of freedom and equality clash. This is, to speak plainly, a hard pill to swallow, and denial of this reality is widespread. How do we deal with both the reality and the denial? Fishkin (in Pojman and Westmoreland 1997:155) argues:

> Equal opportunity is a useful test case for contemporary liberalism. First, it provides an area of social choice where major substantive commitments of liberalism inevitably clash, even for ideal theory. Hence, it should affect our conception of the appropriate connections between ideal theory and the real world of policy prescriptions. It should discredit the model according to which we make asymptotic approaches to a single, unified, and coherent ideal. Rather, we have conflicting principles, any one of which, if given further emphasis, would take policy in a different direction.

Even for the best of circumstances, we have to balance conflicting principles. We are left with ideals without an ideal.

We know that these inconsistencies and conflicts among our ideals exist, because they repeatedly arise in substantive policy debates. Debates about public policy in liberal democracies are often about the contradiction between freedom and equality. The implicit goal is to find some compromise that entails acceptable restrictions and tolerable trade-offs.

Freedom of Speech in Canada

One basic issue in which the contradiction between freedom and equality appears clearly is free speech. Advocates of freedom argue that people should have a right to free expression and should not under any circumstances be restricted in or punished for the public expression of ideas, however unpopular or unattractive to some or many. In recent times particularly, advocates of equality have argued that speech that demeans any human group or category of people—such as women, gays, people of color, Jews, Poles, Scots, and so forth—undermines equality and must be banned. Criticisms, condemnations, and even jokes about groups and categories should, say advocates of collective equality, be banned.

Some countries, such as Canada, have indeed passed so-called "hate speech" laws that ban statements that would be deemed offensive and have imposed severe penalties upon those convicted. As well, the Government of Canada and the governments of a number of the provinces have established Human Rights Commissions to hear complaints, give judgments, and assess penalties for human rights abuses, such as discrimination in hiring for jobs, renting housing, etc., on the basis of race, ethnicity, religion, gender, and sexual orientation. Many of these commissions are charged with clauses against discriminatory opinion (O'Neill 2008:A12):

> Section 7 of B.C.'s [British Columbia's] human rights act makes it an offence for any person to publish "a statement, publication, notice, sign, symbol, emblem or other representation" that so much as "indicates discrimination or an intention to discriminate" against a protected group, or "is likely to expose a person or group or a class of persons to hatred or contempt." No actual discrimination or hatred has to occur for an offence to occur. And . . . truth is not a defence.

The Canadian Human Rights act says, in section 12, much the same, but adds a neat specification:

> Furthermore, Section 13 makes it an offence for anyone "to communicate telephonically [a definition that includes the internet] . . . any matter that is likely to expose a person or persons to hatred or contempt."

Once again, "freedom of speech," "freedom of opinion," "freedom of the press," "fair comment," and "true information" are not allowable defenses. Furthermore, the Human Rights Commissions are notoriously lacking in due process, for there are no strict rules of evidence, the accused cannot face his accuser, and the investigators and commissioners make no claim to neutrality, for they are committed activists on behalf of the "victims" of discrimination. If all that is not dire enough, complaints can be submitted cost free, while defendants must pay their costs, often for years of adjudication.

To illustrate, let us briefly review the case of a Christian pastor who was prosecuted for saying that homosexuality is a sin (Levant 2007:A16). He had sent a letter to the *Red Deer Advocate* newspaper expressing his view, and in response a local teacher complained to the Alberta Human Rights Commission. The Commissioner ruled that "the publication's exposure of homosexuals to hatred and contempt trumps the freedom of speech afforded in the [Canadian] Charter [of Rights]." As Levant (2007:A16) says:

> That was it: Freedom of speech, and of the press, and religion, all of which are called "fundamental freedoms" in our Constitution, now come second to the newly discovered right of a thin-skinned bystander not to be offended.

But we mustn't think that these commissions are mavericks running wild; on the contrary, provincial governments have been strongly supportive. In the above-mentioned case of the pastor, an Alberta Government lawyer was sent to speak on behalf of the complainant. So too in British Columbia, where the New Democratic Party (NDP) Government considered expanding the act to criminalize criticism of abortionists (O'Neill 2008:A12).

The Human Rights Commissions had had a pretty free pass as they established their modus operandi and prosecuted a variety of small fry. But that changed when they took up complaints against more influential people and institutions. (There might be a parallel here with Senator Joseph McCarthy's anti-communist crusade during the late 1940s–1950s, which played havoc with many individuals' lives, until he started making accusations against the U.S. Army. He got nowhere, and was censured by the Senate.) In one case, a complaint was made against Ezra Levant for publishing the Danish cartoons of Mohammed in the paper he edited, the *Western Standard* (Levant 2008:A13). In the other case, a complaint was made against *Maclean's,* the Canadian national news magazine, for publishing an excerpt of renown journalist Mark Steyn's *America Alone* that describes the demographic explosion of Muslims in Europe (Levant 2007:A16). In these cases, the tribunals had hooked big fish that were ready to defend themselves and were capable of fighting. Levant (2008:A13; 2009:ch. 7) began his hearing with a "statement," a lengthy treatise on the reasons that the Alberta Human Rights Commission had no right to act as censors, was unconstitutional, and was violating Levant's human rights. This statement was published in newspapers (Levant 2008:A13), on Levant's website (ezralevant.com), on YouTube (http://www.youtube.com/watch?v=AzVJTHIvqw8), and the interrogation that followed was recorded and put up on YouTube, becoming an instant hit (for one of several segments: http://www.youtube.com/watch?v=3iMNM1tef7g). According to Leonard Stern (2008:B6), editorial pages editor of the *Ottawa Citizen*, "The confrontation between Calgary journalist Ezra Levant and the Alberta human rights commission is now the stuff of Canadian legend. . . . Mr. Levant is now a folk hero to those who are fed up with bullying human rights commissions." Eventually, at considerable cost—in time, energy, and legal fees—to the defendants, the cases against Levant and *Maclean's* were dismissed.

The Canadian and provincial human rights commissions were established to advance and defend the equality of treatment and equality of respect for the citizens of Canada and the provinces. These goals are widely supported in Canada. Complainants in the *Maclean's* case—law students Muneeza Sheikh, Naseem Mithoowani, Khurrum Awan, Daniel Simard, and Ali Ahmed—argued that they were trying to draw attention to an "Islamophobic bias" in *Maclean's* articles (Sheikh et al. 2007:A11).

At the same time, the rights of free speech and free press are well established in Canadian constitutional law. As Levant (2008:A13; see also 2009:ch. 7) pointed out in his Alberta Human Rights Commission hearing:

> The 1960 Canadian Bill of Rights guaranteed: "human rights and fundamental freedoms, namely . . . (c) freedom of religion; (d) freedom of speech; (e) freedom of assembly and association; and (f) freedom of the press."

> In 1982, the Canadian charter of Rights and Freedoms guaranteed that "Everyone has the following fundamental freedoms: (a) freedom of conscience and religion; (b) freedom of thought, belief, opinion and expression, including freedom of the press and other media of communication."

These values are also widely supported by Canadian public opinion. And by the above-mentioned constitutional documents, are guaranteed.

Obviously there is a conflict between a mandate that requires restriction of speech, press, and expression on behalf of equality of respect and suppression of discrimination, on the one hand, and, on the other hand, a mandate that legitimizes freedom of thought, speech, press, and communication. In this situation, equality means restriction of expression, while freedom allows full expression. There is no simple way to resolve this contradiction.

Freedom of Education

A second common and recurring issue is public versus private education. Advocates of public education stress equality in education, even to the point of suppressing or even denying differences in educability among children and insisting on providing the same to all. Some supporters of public education would effectively, if not explicitly, ban private educational institutions. Many advocates of private education demand that decisions about education reside in families, and that families must have choice in educational options and the right to send children to private institutions, which, they believe, provide better education and safer environments. Further debates on this topic are whether all citizens must support public schools even if neither they nor their families use them, so as to support equality, and whether public funds, either applied directly or as subsidies or through tax deductions, should be used to support private educational institutions, so as to support freedom in the allocation of funding.

Schooling issues have played important parts in recent public discussions and in Ontario provincial elections. When the Conservatives under Mike Harris were implementing their "common sense revolution" in Ontario, one of their measures was to give limited tax credit for private school tuition. The reason was that all Ontario taxpayers by law financially support the public school system; parents who send their children to private schools additionally pay private school tuition. As these parents are already doing their civic duty by supporting the public school, those who send their children to private school should have some tax relief for their private tuition costs.

However, when the Liberals under Dalton McGuinty succeeded the Harris Conservatives, they revoked the tax credit for private school tuition. The reason was that parents should not be encouraged by tax relief to send their children to private schools. Private schools, in the view of the Liberals, are sources of separation and inequality. Equality is best served by all students being educated by the same public school system. So while sending children to private school remained legal, the parents would have to carry the full financial burden for private school tuition, in addition to their share of the cost of public schools. It did not pass unnoticed, however, that Ontario's special arrangements made the Catholic school system into a public school system, funded entirely by taxes. This apparently suited Liberal Premier McGuinty, who had gone to Catholic school, who sends his children to Catholic school, and whose wife teaches in Catholic school.

During the last Ontario provincial election, held in October 2007, the Conservative leader John Tory saw an advantage in a policy that changed school funding. Let's be fair, he said; if Catholic schools are funded, so should Jewish, Muslim, Hindu, and other religious schools.

That, he suggested, would be true equality. But the voters hated this idea, because of fear that supporting religious schools would lead to greater separation among citizens, and, more specifically, because voters were afraid—although no one ever admitted it outright—that Islamic schools would lead to extremism and terrorism. The Conservatives were drubbed; the Liberals were reelected handily; and John Tory resigned as leader of the Conservatives (Gillespie 2007).

The most recent debate on schooling in Ontario resulted when it became known that new policies mandated that students would not be penalized for late papers or for plagiarism, and that no student would fail, but all would be promoted, no matter what his or her academic performance. These policies followed earlier ones outlawing the separation of strong students, weak students, and disabled students into different streams, thus insuring a mix of all types of students in each classroom, on the grounds that all students should be treated equally. With the new regulations, good, poor, and no academic performance were to be treated equally.

Not all teachers, parents, students, and commentators were delighted with this triumph of equality. Editorials, op-eds, and letters to the editor flowed throughout Ontario and beyond. These measures were said to be in conflict with achievement, excellence, and common sense. They are "dumbing down" our schools, came the cry. This is madness, they continued, in a world of international competition. For those holding these opinions, measures advancing equality could be overdone.

A new twist in the debate about education has arisen with regard to French immersion education in Canada. French and English are the two official languages of Canada, and their use is mandated in government services. This means that many jobs in the federal government are bilingual, and capability in both official languages is important for provincial positions and business. Therefore educating young people in both official languages is desirable, both for their job prospects as well as for the integration of French and English sectors in Canada. Usually anglophones and allophones are not admitted to French school systems, but rather are directed to French immersion schools in English school systems. The idea, of course, is that they will graduate capable in both their English and French, to the benefit of all.

However, participation in French immersion programs, as compared with full English schooling, has turned out to be skewed (O'Toole 2009:A8). Studies from across Canada, including those from Statistics Canada, indicate that students in French immersion programs were from more affluent families, while those in full English programs were from poorer families. Furthermore, the stronger, more capable students were in the immersion program, while weaker students, including special needs students, stuck to the basic English program. French immersion programs therefore are seen as contributing to class and capability differentials. Advocates of equality see this undesired and unexpected effect of immersion programs to be unjust and unconscionable.

In the first case described, tax credits for private school tuition, the conflicting values are equality and freedom to allocate one's resources where one likes. In the second case, public funding of separate religious schools, equality of treatment is opposed overtly by unity, commonality, and, to use the French term, fraternité, and covertly by security concerns. In the third case, treating all students equally, the opposition is between equality and achievement.

Freedom of Medical Care

A third major issue is public versus private medical care. Advocates of a public system of medical care, and of equality, argue that all people by virtue of being human beings have a right to medical care and that differences in wealth should not determine medical-care sufficiency. Advocates of private health care, and of freedom, say that people should have a right to allocate their resources as they see fit, and to allocate them to private health care if they are not satisfied with public health care. This is a major public debate in Canada today, and these issues are part of the health-care reform controversy in the US as well. For more than three decades Canada has had a universal health-care system that, in contrast with the American private system, has become a, if not the, central element in Canadian identity and a source of great pride to many Canadians and a source of envy to some American politicians.

However, the Canadian system has increasingly become ineffective in delivering treatment, at the same time as its costs have skyrocketed: people might spend months or even years on waiting lists even for major procedures and critical treatments, and some types of equipment are scarce or outdated or both. In 2009, in the eastern medical administrative region of Ontario, which contains Ottawa, the capital of Canada, the average wait for an Magnetic Resonance Imaging (MRI) scan was 240 days, twice the Ontario average, which was "only" 120 days. The wait must seem long if you are wondering if you have cancer. But if you want a definitive test of whether you have cancer, you need a Positron Emission Tomography (PET) scan. Unfortunately, PET scans are not readily available in Ontario. The Provincial medical system does not pay for them, so no hospitals give them. If you want an MRI or PET scan, and are willing to pay for it, around $2000, you must find a rare private clinic in Ontario, go to a private clinic in Quebec, or go to the US.

The significance of access to PET scans is illustrated by the following case. After eight months of grueling colon cancer treatment, Howard Steinberg had an unpleasant surprise: a diagnosis that the malignancy had spread (Blackwell 2009:A1). Two large tumors were in his liver and required further chemotherapy or surgery, both potentially dangerous. Steinberg decided that he wanted further confirmation. He found a "little-known" private clinic in Mississauga, a suburb of Toronto, where he got a PET scan. To his happy surprise, the PET scan found that he was cancer free, a result confirmed by additional tests. So he did not have to undergo further treatment. The Mississauga clinic is planning to expand its service to Windsor, Ontario. But elsewhere in Ontario, PET scans are not available. The lack of access to PET scans can also mean that cancers go untreated. Blackwell (2009:A8) reports:

> Dr. Jean-Luc Urbain, who practiced in his native Belgium and the United States before settling in London, Ont., said he has never seen as many advanced cancers as he has in Canada, and suspects the lack of PET scan service is to blame. "Ontario has been in total denial," he charges.

Canadian supporters of the public system argue that in the Canadian system, which, uniquely with Cuba and North Korea bans private medical care, everyone has an equal chance of receiving or not receiving medical care, and that *equality* is of paramount importance. But what this means, in practice, is that while your mother must wait 18 months for a hip operation, your dog can have a hip operation next week. As Mark Steyn (2000:A18) impolitely put it, "Universal lack of access [to treatment]. Equality of crap." However, in June 2005, the Supreme Court of Canada, rather to the surprise of all, ruled that medical treatment delayed is medical treatment denied, that such denial violates the right of security of the person, and that in such circumstances laws that forbid private treatment are unconstitutional. This decision has inspired a current lawsuit brought by a number of private clinics, including one owned by Dr. Brian Day, the past president of the Canadian Medical Association, arguing that it is unconstitutional to bar Canadians access to private medical treatment, and thus to the freedom to use their resources as they like (Blackwell 2009:A8). The debate continues.

Liberal Democracies: Discussion

These examples—and others, such as mandatory membership in trade unions—indicate that, in societies that value them both, the contradiction between equality and freedom is a constant source of discontent, debate, and conflict, even in societies such as Canada, which deems itself skilled in compromise. Those who hold to either equality or freedom as a dominant principle, cathecting it above all others, will constantly be dissatisfied with public policy that compromises, according to majoritarian views, to accommodate the other principle. Such policy compromises will never be tidy or elegant and will always be a source of discontent to visionaries. Fishkin (in Pojman and Westmorland 1997:157–158) argues that absolutist commitment to either equality or freedom, "combined with the inevitable conflicts and indeterminacies of liberalism," leads liberal society to a crisis of legitimacy. "The ingredients are the clash between expectations and inevitable limits." Fishkin's conclusion is:

> Either we must learn to expect less, or liberalism undermines itself as a coherent moral ideality. My solution is to jettison the absolutist expectations and to embrace, by contrast, a limited liberalism. . . . We do not need a *systematic* theory and the demand for one is a part of the problem.

In spite of entertaining conflicting values and contradictory goals, liberal democracies have in general succeeded sufficiently in compromise and balancing to satisfy majorities or at least pluralities of their citizens. True, electoral politics, in seesaw fashion, places in power advocates of one approach only to replace them with advocates of a contradictory approach. In Ontario, for example, the moderate Progressive Conservatives were replaced by the socialist New Democratic Party (NDP), who were shortly thereafter succeeded by harder-line conservatives and their Common Sense Revolution (CSR), which dismantled many NDP policies and which itself was succeeded by the Liberals, who dismantled CSR policies. But it is precisely this see-saw, with its trials of different mixes through alternatives presented by different parties, that provides citizens of liberal democracies options from which to select their preferred mix and keeps them moderately contented while selecting. Liberal democracy may be a particularly messy system of governance, while at the same time being the most satisfying for its citizens.

Nothing is more normal than that people desire various things and wish to have all of the things that they desire. But reality is often not compliant; the means available frequently are not sufficient to achieve the desired ends. We also know that our budgets may stretch to a new car or a new patio or a new boat, but not all three and not even two. We have to choose one and forgo, for the time being, the others. We also know that, given limited time, motivation, energy, and intelligence, we cannot, except for the very rare individual, be philosophers, doctors, lawyers, and rocket scientists in one lifetime.

Furthermore, choices always have consequences, sometimes unintended consequences. We know this from our private lives. If we use our funds to buy a high end music system, we will have to forgo a new wardrobe. If we buy a new car, our overseas vacation will have to be postponed. More significantly, if we do our degrees in social science and humanities, we shall not be able to pursue qualification as a veterinarian or engineer.

What is true in our personal and family lives is also true in our collective lives. Community norms and public policy, aimed at achieving certain collective desiderata, are also limited by their means and also have consequences, sometimes inadvertent and undesired. The simple case is use of public funds. If we subsidize sports but not the arts, then our capacity in arts will be lessened and our culture less enriched by the arts. If we fund professional sports alone, we may forgo the health benefits of amateur sports; but if we fund only amateur sports, our standing among the nations will be diminished.

Perhaps more seriously, if, in order to advance equality, we heavily tax those with substantial income to redistribute funds to those with less income, we may find that investment in the economy suffers, the economy does not advance or even shrinks, innovation is reduced, and jobs are not created. Here we aim to assist those less well-off and to advance equality but suffer the consequence, unintended and perhaps unrecognized or denied, of a weak economy and a shift from work to state dependence. As well, if we wish to be peacemakers rather than warriors, as was the policy of Canada during the 1980s and 1990s, and so publically laud peacekeeping and disparage military conflict, and reduce greatly the defense budget, then with the occurrence of bellicose threat or military conflict, we are not in a position to respond militarily and must depend upon others to defend us, or else capitulate to any threatening opposition. In general, our knowledge is imperfect and incomplete, and consequences may be unknown, denied, or advocated. But consequences there will be to choices, and this cannot be avoided.

FREEDOM AND EQUALITY: CONCLUSION

In this chapter we have reviewed philosophical, anthropological, and historical material pertinent to considering the relationship between freedom and equality. We focused on individual freedom in the sense of not being interfered with by others, and economic equality. Although there are many astute philosophical discussions about individual freedom and economic equality, and their relationship, conclusions tend to be drawn on the basis of reasoning and thought experiments. We have tried to expand the universe of information relevant to this question by examining a number of societies described in the ethnographic and historical record. By doing so, we have attempted to shed further light on what appears to be possible in the real world, as evidenced by what people have accomplished. When people have implemented a policy of advancing freedom or equality, or found themselves in circumstances favoring one or the other, what are the consequences? This is what we have tried to document in our review of cases.

In segmentary societies, tribes, such as the Bedouin, Somali, Baluch, Turkmen, Nuer, and Pakhtuns, where order is maintained by balanced opposition of groups, and "self-help," with all men required

to be warriors, group solidarity is a strong value and a practical necessity. Tribesmen are convinced that their security interests coincide
with their fellow group members, and that their most important
resource is support from their fellows. For this reason, good relations
with a wide range of kin, a sense of well-being among kin, and cohesion among kin are high priorities. Kin group solidarity in a tribal
context means strong political support, readiness to fight on behalf of
one's kin. But it means more than that; it means looking out for the
welfare of kin, helping out kin, "being there" for them in any time of
need or difficulty. This is manifested in economic as well as social and
psychological support; people's material resources are shared with
their kin. In many ways, some specified by custom and some faculta-
tive, goods and services are exchanged or redistributed in ways that
aid those in need. People invest in other people, their kin. Generosity
that distributes goods and services advances and supports economic
equality, and equality supports group solidarity, which is the best
guarantee of security. At the same time, there is a high level of individual freedom, extending to movement, residence, work patterns,
and allocation of important capital resources, such as livestock. The
coincidence of considerable economic equality and substantial individual freedom results from the voluntary nature of economic redistribution of goods and labor. Voluntary generalized reciprocity is a
consequence of the collective, kin group based security system.

Corporate societies, such as the communities of the highland
Latin America and highland Sardinia, and states such as Cuba, the
Soviet Union, and Communist China, also stress solidarity, unity, and
equality as necessary support for cohesion. Economic differentiation is
seen as the driver of wedges among people, and thus the enemy of fraternity, brotherhood, and unity. Differences in wealth are forbidden,
and the community and state are given the role of holder of collective
wealth and enforcer of equality. Capital resources, economic activities,
and the occupational structure are controlled by the community or
state, as is any "surplus" economic accumulation. Freedom of association, of movement, of economic enterprise, are restricted if not forbidden. Because the rules of economic equality are imposed rather than
being voluntary, political and coercive controls are applied to the population. Freedom of speech, of the press, of political participation, of emi-
gration are all so limited that it is accurate to say these freedoms do not
exist. Economic equality is enforced at the cost of individual liberty. As
well, political inequality becomes the norm, as functionaries of the
state and "the party" monopolize power, leaving none for the citizens,
or, more correctly, the subjects of the corporate state.

Market-based liberal democratic societies, such as Canada and the
United States, and those of the European Union and of Scandinavia,
place high value on both equality and freedom. And while it is true that

historically "equality" was seen primarily in legal and political terms, streams of socialist thought, and, more recently, related ideas of "social justice" and an ever expansive concept of "human rights" have spurred support for economic equality. The traditional notion of freedom as lack of interference, called the "negative" concept of freedom by Isaiah Berlin (1969), has been challenged by a "positive" concept of freedom, which focuses on the societal-supplied capability to do a variety of things. As capability can be seen to require resources, and resources that are not equally distributed to all are not available for some, "positive freedom" and equality conceptually converge. The difficulty that arises, as we have seen in corporate societies, is that economic equality results in the loss of "negative" freedom, freedom from interference, freedom to pursue one's ends as one might. Positive freedom is promised as a result of equality, but the result in practice is a loss of negative individual freedom and the ongoing and intrusive interference of community and state operatives who end up controlling people's lives.

However, advocates of positive freedom have not had their way with market-based liberal democracies. While the value of equality, especially legal and political equality, is strongly held, so too is the value of freedom, both economic and political. A sense of public spirit and a desire for a humane society have supported the advance of economic equality, but in a moderate fashion. In practice, the values of equality and freedom conflict in a variety of public issues, such as speech, schooling, medicine, taxes, government grants, etc., and mainstream political and public policies reflect compromise positions balancing equality and freedom. Rather than aiming for full equality or full freedom, these compromises accept partial degrees of equality and degrees of freedom. Policies in various jurisdictions tend to seesaw a bit over time, favoring equality a bit more under one administration, favoring a bit more freedom under a different administration. The electorate favors an emphasis on equality at one time, then, gets fed up with the policies it generates, and revises in favor of an emphasis on freedom. Over time, both values are maintained, and both are compromised to a degree. Is there a better solution?

Our comparative study supports Isaiah Berlin's (1969) view that we cannot put into practice at one time all social values. (More incompatibilities would arise if we consider other values such as creativity, honor, brotherhood, purity, prosperity, godliness, and diversity.) Thus political promises that, if we are willing to sacrifice now, we can succeed at achieving all of these values together, are illusory and likely to lead to disaster. Second, the investigation presented here suggests that important values such as "equality" and "freedom" are legitimate and useful subjects of anthropological investigation, and that anthropologists have substantial ethnographic resources to bring to bear on their study. Third, notwithstanding contemporary cavils about "master discourses," and denials of the possibility of general and valid knowledge, our understanding that not all values and goals are compatible is an example of a viable and general formulation about the way the world works.

ILLUSTRATIVE COMPARISONS

Comparing contrasting cases assists us in grasping the significance of differences. In chapter 3, we examined Benedict's markedly contrasting premises of three different cultures, and the consequent spirits of the three; Wolf's similar treatment of open and closed peasant communities; Lévi-Strauss' demonstration that, in aid of social integration, two societies can take apparently opposite measures; Geertz's observations of the remarkably different spirits of Indonesian and Moroccan Islam and how these are tied to contrasting environments, ways of making a living, and social relations; and Edgerton's generalizations across distinct tribal cultures about the contrasting characters of farmers and pastoralists. In this chapter, Salzman has argued that different societies having civil peace can implement either freedom or equality, but not both. Juxtaposing intellectually contrasting cases such as these places us in a stronger position to understand and explain the differences between or among them, and to identify, as Nadel has recommended, those invariant relationships between factors that are constants in building societies and cultures.

Chapter Five

Controlled Comparisons

Controlled comparisons are made between societies or cultures that have many similarities, such that the differences that do exist can be seen to be related to other differences present. The similarities can be considered "control factors," in that similarities cannot be used to explain differences, which must be explained by, or at least related to, other differences.

WITCHCRAFT

Anthropologists studying "witchcraft" have taken as their main foci the cultural manifestation of witchcraft beliefs, on the one hand, and, on the other, the social manifestation of witchcraft accusations. Both beliefs and patterns of accusation differ from society to society, culture to culture. The question of why these manifestations vary between closely related communities is taken up by S. F. Nadel in his article, "Witchcraft in Four African Societies" (1952).

The Nupe and Gwari, close neighbors in northern Nigeria, live in similar environments and are in close contact. They speak related languages and have similar kinship, ritual, and political systems. The economies of the two are similar, except that trading in markets is much more important among the Nupe. Their beliefs in witchcraft are virtually identical. "Both conceive of witchcraft as unequivocally evil, as destroying life, mainly through mysterious wasting diseases, and as implying the power of witches to 'eat' the 'life-soul' of their victims" (Nadel 1952:18). Witches' spirits travel away from their bodies, and so are impossible to observe, and thus to prove or disprove.

But there is one very clear difference among the Nupe and Gwari in witchcraft beliefs and accusations: For the Gwari, witches may be men or may be women; there is no distinction in this regard along sex lines. In contrast, among the Nupe, witches are always women, those accused of witchcraft are always women, and it is common that older women are thought to use their witching powers to victimize young men. Men, among the Nupe, are thought to be benevolent and to withhold help to female witches. Indeed, it is Nupe's male secret society that is thought to be the best defense against witchcraft, using threats and torture to cleanse villages of witchcraft.

How can this difference between Nupe and Gwari be explained? Nadel (1952:28) argues that, in general, witchcraft beliefs reflect "specific anxieties and stress arising in social life." Among the Nupe, the major stresses in social relations arise in marriage, between husbands and wives. While husbands apply themselves to agriculture, the women often leave the village to engage in itinerant trading. The profits sometimes leave them better off financially than their husbands. Furthermore, women traders, traveling alone away from their husbands, are thought to engage in illicit sexual relations. By so doing, they are abandoning their household, their children, and of course their husbands. As Nadel (1952:21) explains it, "the men must submit to the domineering and independent leanings of the women; they resent their own helplessness, and definitely blame the 'immorality' of the women-folk." The hostility between men and women and the desire of men to change the situation are projected into the witchcraft beliefs and accusations. It is indicative that the woman believed to be the head witch is the titled, official head of the women traders! It is also consistent that witches are thought to be older women victimizing younger men. Men feel themselves to be the victims of independent, dominating women, who attack them and eat their "life-souls." While men dare not challenge their independent and well-off wives, they can speak out strongly against the immoral, female witches.

Among the Gwari, there is no such antagonism between the sexes or between the spouses. Trading plays a much smaller part in the Gwari economy, and both husband and wife are more focused on the household and on cultivation. Marriages tend to be tension-free, and there is no general antipathy between the sexes. Therefore witches are conceived of indifferently as men and women, and tensions from which accusations arise would be more individualistic than structural.

The second comparison that Nadel makes is between the Korongo and Mesakin of central Sudan. The two tribes are neighbors in the same environment and have the same economy, political system, and religion. Both trace descent through the female line and have the same kinship and domestic systems. An important relationship in both is that between the sister's son and the mother's brother, from whom the sister's son inherits. Many boys, about 50 percent in each tribe, leave their fathers' houses at age six or seven and move in with their mothers' brothers.

Like many southern Sudanese and East African societies, the men in these tribes are organized into age sets, groups defined by age that go through a defined sequence of age grades with activities and restrictions appropriate for each grade. In both societies, competitive sports—light wrestling, heavy wrestling, and spear fighting—are associated with particular age grades and are deemed manifestations of manly vigor.

A striking difference between these two very similar tribes is the absence of witchcraft in one and its major significance in the other. Nadel (1952:23) explains:

> The Korongo have no witchcraft beliefs at all; the Mesakin are literally obsessed by fears of witchcraft and witchcraft accusations, entailing violent quarrels, assaults, and blood revenge, are frequent. Witchcraft itself is a mysterious, malignant and often deadly power, emanating directly from evil wishes. . . . Mesakin witchcraft is believed to operate only between maternal kin, especially between a mother's brother and sister's son, the older relative assailing the younger.

What lies behind the tension between mother's brother (MB) and sister's son (ZS) is inheritance. More specifically, it is anticipatory inheritance: demand of the ZS for an animal from the herd of the MB, from whom he will eventually inherit. Among the Korongo, this demand does not lead to great tension; the gift can be postponed, but eventually it is given with more or less good grace. Not, however, among the Mesakin, where the request for an animal from the ZS is taken as an affront, and refused. But the animal must be given, although sometimes the ZS just takes one. The MB feels great resentment toward the ZS. Should the ZS fall ill, it is assumed by all that he has fallen to the MB's witchcraft. But no one is surprised; all older men know what the MB was feeling.

How can we understand the difference in response from the Korongo MB and the Mesakin MB? Nadel traces the difference to the differences in the age-grade systems in the two tribes. The Korongo have six age grades, including one for men aged 26–50, which includes for its earlier years spear fighting and visits to cattle camps. The final category for those 50 and above is for old men. The Mesakin age-grade system has only three grades—boy, man, old man—the old man category beginning at age 26. So while Korongo men in their 20s and 30s can engage in activities of male prowess, Mesakin men of that age have been declared old men who have lost their male vigor. So when a Mesakin's ZS approaches his MB and says, since you are still alive, at least give me one animal as anticipatory inheritance, the MB is far from ready to accept his old man status and is angry that the ZS is throwing it in his face. This resentment is what lies behind witchcraft accusations:

> The hostility which, one knows, the older man feels but should not feel, and which he has no means of realising finally and successfully, is accepted as operating in the sphere of secret as well as antisocial aims, that is, in the sphere of witchcraft. Every man projects his own frustrations of this nature into the allegations that others are guilty of witchcraft. In punishing them, the accuser vicariously wipes out his own guilt, unadmitted or admitted. (Nadel 1952:26)

FATHER'S BROTHER'S DAUGHTER MARRIAGE

For many students of anthropology, discussions of kinship appear to be pointless excursions into unnecessary detail. But in the many societies that use kinship as their idiom for social organization, it is a vital matter that touches on their hopes and fears, and their life chances. Fredrik Barth's study of "Father's Brother's Daughter Marriage in Kurdistan" (1970[1954]) shows that marriages among the Kurds are used strategically in order to form political alliances, which serve to secure peaceful relations and access to material resources.

The Kurds of Kirkuk and Suleimani in northern Iraq, like Kurds in Iran and Turkey, occupy several kinds of environment: mountain villages, towns in valleys, and cities. The mountain Kurds, like the mountain Berbers of North Africa and the mountain Pakhtuns of Afghanistan, have segmentary societies, rather like the Nuer, Somali, and Bedouin discussed in chapter 4. Groups of descendants from common ancestors through the male line have the responsibility of providing security, including protecting the land and defending against any attack. Among themselves, in their mountain villages, small subgroups of kinsmen—brothers, sons, and cousins—struggle with equivalent groups for political power, which largely rests on the number of riflemen in the group. The first line of possible schism is between cousins. Senior men trying to maintain or advance their political power will strive to secure the alliance and loyalty of brothers' sons, the cousins of their sons. How do they do this?

Among the Kurds, the Bedouin, and many other Middle Eastern peoples, there is a norm, or rule, that a man has the right to marry his father's brother's daughter, and he must be willing to renounce that right if the girl is to legitimately marry someone else. There is also a custom that when paternal cousins wed, the bride-price (another term for bridewealth)—ordinarily substantial—paid by the groom is largely reduced or waived entirely. Now when a young man marries his father's brother's daughter, his father's brother becomes his father-in-law, and his male cousins become his brothers-in-law. The potential split between cousins is thus bridged by these in-law ties. As Barth (1970[1954]:133) puts it:

> If a man alienates his nephews by refusing them their traditional rights [to marry his daughters], he loses their political support. If he, on the other hand, gives them his daughters in marriage, the ties are reinforced and lineage solidarity maintained. The girl's father creates an obligation on the part of his brother's son to give him political support by exempting him from paying the bride-price.

It is for this reason that many Kurdish villagers, if they have the requisite number of daughters at the appropriate ages, will give them to their brothers' sons. Barth found, in two mountain villages, that from 21 marriages, nine, or 43 percent, were between brothers' children, three with other cousins, three with other relatives, two with unrelated villagers, and four with other villages.

However, not all Kurdish people live in mountain villages organized by segmentary lineages. Those who live in more feudally organized territory, such as that adjacent to the mountain region of the Kurds just described, have greater emphasis on land ownership and class. The norm of paternal cousin marriage is not as stressed, and bride-prices are lower in all categories. Furthermore, and most tellingly, actual paternal cousin marriage is at a much lower level than in the mountains: of 46 marriages, six, or 13 percent, were paternal cousins, two were other cousins, nine other relatives, 19 were unrelated villagers, and ten from other villages. This substantial drop in paternal cousin marriages in the feudal area suggests that high rates of cousin marriage were related to the segmentary lineage organization in the mountain villages. Another way to say this is that, in the mountains, men's strategic decision making led them to favor paternal cousin marriage, while in the feudal communities, men's strategic interests did not lead them to emphasize paternal cousin marriage. Barth (1970[1954]:136) sums it up: The "pattern of father's brother's daughter marriage plays a prominent role in solidifying the minimal lineage as a corporate group in factional struggle."

AGRICULTURAL EVOLUTION

Native peoples in the southwestern desert of Arizona had adapted to the environment through a combination of wet agriculture and hunting and gathering. Although these natives were very similar in physical type, language, and material culture, those natives who lived in the arid intermontane valleys and who relied to some extent on agriculture but more heavily on hunting and gathering, from Spanish times came to be called Papago, while those who lived in the valley of the substantial Gila River, and who relied more heavily on agriculture, came to be called Pima. The Papago relied on scattered springs for water, and scattered fields for agriculture, usually depending on rainwater from runoff channels to water their crops. They lived for the most part in family groups and were nomadic, migrating between their various springs and cultivated fields. But they gained more than 75 percent of their food from hunting and gathering. The Pima, in contrast, received a good summer crop from the fields irrigated by the Gila River and relied on wild plants and animals for around 40 percent of their foodstuffs. They resided permanently in nucleated villages, some dozen extending 55 miles along the river valley. The different ways of life of the Papago and Pima were more matters of different emphases from the same repertoire of activities and arrangements.

Robert A. Hackenberg in "Economic Alternatives in Arid Lands: A Case Study of the Pima and Papago Indians" (1962) interrogates this case to illuminate the sources of economic development or evolution. He compares two native populations, but also compares the two over time, exploring different historical periods looking for the springs and consequences of change. In this way he offers a double comparison.

A major impetus to change was the arrival of winter wheat with the Spanish. Winter wheat allowed the Pima, who had previously relied solely on summer corn (maize), to cultivate year-round and to forgo reliance on hunting and gathering altogether. The Papago, however, could not consolidate their fields and water sources to produce a crop sufficient to fill their needs. Another major impetus to change was the challenge presented by the Apache wars, which required major defensive innovations. The Papago built some defensive forts but could not live in them regularly, as they had to continue with their nomadic movement. The Pima, however, were able, now that they could rely totally on their crops, to consolidate, both physically and politically. The Pima shifted their villages from a 55-mile stretch into a more concentrated 12-mile stretch. Several villages had common canal systems. A supravillage structure formed under a common chief and a tribal system of defense. As the economy grew and surpluses were produced, the Pima hired Papago laborers, signaling a developing social differentiation.

However, despite their advancement, the Pima were not able to recover from the drought of 1854 and the flood of 1868, or to effectively adopt the new industrial agriculture of the Euro-American society that came to surround them. Twentieth-century government-sponsored agricultural development projects among the Pima have not succeeded, and the natives have mostly ended up as agricultural laborers in American industrial agricultural enterprises. Hackenburg (1962) argues that the Pima had not developed their organization sufficiently to adopt industrial agriculture, as irrigation farmers in some countries, such as Burma and Thailand, have been able to do.

ACHIEVEMENT MOTIVATION AND DEVELOPMENT

We all know students who are focused on their studies, dedicated to doing well, committed to putting in the effort needed, and we all know students who, while they might like to do well in their studies, find it hard to crack those books, find it hard to reject an invitation to go out for a beer or to a party, and just don't quite get in gear to study for exams or to write those essays. We all know professors who are well prepared for their lectures, dedicated to their research and publishing, and always willing to help with administrative tasks. And there are professors—none of my colleagues to be sure—who are not prepared for classes, do not get much research done, and are not around when administrative chores need to be done. One way we think about this is motivation: good students and professors are strongly motivated to achieve; the others, not so much. Looking more widely at larger populations, countries, and regions, some of which are developing impressively, while others seem to languish without progress, we might wonder to what extent differences in motivation play a part in these varying results. This is the question addressed by Robert LeVine in *Dreams and Deeds: Achievement Motivation in Nigeria* (1966), a comparative study in psychological anthropology with some parallels to Edgerton's *The Individual in Cultural Adaptation* (1971), notably the placing of psychological factors within a wider social and cultural context, the use of projective tests, and the quantitative assessment of the test results.

All peoples, all cultures, value success. It could hardly be otherwise, as success is simply fulfilling the values and ideals of a culture. However, and this is particularly interesting for students of culture, all cultures, not having the same ideals and values, do not have the same definitions of success. Some cultures have other worldly definitions of success, such as the traditional Indian emphasis on fulfilling one's duty and one's destiny, usually limited to an inherited task, the Burmese emphasis on investing in prayers by supporting monks and building temples, or the encouragement of martyrs in Palestine. Some cultures define success as conquest, such as the Romans, Arabs, Mongols, and Europeans at certain periods of history. Another definition, widespread in stable, agrarian societies is defining success in terms of nonworking status. Because bone-breaking and life-draining physical labor is necessary for most people to survive in agrarian societies, being able to avoid such work by having others work for you is an unmistakable sign of high status. In many African cultures—but, as we shall see, this varies from culture to culture and group to group—"conspicuous leisure" is the primary manifestation of status. And so, as LeVine (1966:4) says, "it is by demonstration of the power to command the labor of others that a person maintains his status in the public eye." Many Africans work very hard, in many situations must do so, but hard work is undertaken because it is necessary, not because it is valued. What is valued is to avoid work, but most cannot manage to do so. These values contrast with current Western values. According to LeVine (1966:8):

> The point of greatest contrast is self-reliance, since the Western ideal of achieving excellence on a person's own runs counter to the African notion that self-reliance involves displaying a humiliating lack of social power.

But some African groups have values closer to the Western norm. In Nigeria, the locus of LeVine's (1966:8) study:

> The Ibo are the energetic parvenus who in a few decades altered the established order, both by successfully challenging Yoruba supremacy in the professional and civil service elite and by leading the struggle for Nigerian nationalism which led to independence from Britain.

The other main groups that LeVine studies are the Hausa and Yoruba.

- "The Hausa are the 'backwoods' politicians: conservative, religiously orthodox (Islam), with little formal education or urban sophistication, but with the largest bloc of votes in their control and a well-developed sense of practical power politics" (LeVine 1966:7).

- "The Yoruba are the most urbane group, with the longest history of Westernization, Christianity, and education" (LeVine 1966:7).

LeVine's research focuses on the notions of success in these populations, and their average motivation.

Why do different personality characteristics develop in different societies? It seems clear that an individual's psychology exists somewhat separately from societal institutions and their rules: personalities are integrated in individual psychologies, while society is integrated collectively in terms of functional interrelationships, and culture is integrated publically in terms of logic and meaning. However, there must be some degree of fit between individuals and the society and culture they live in, because society and culture can be maintained and reproduced only when individuals willingly conform, at least to a substantial degree. If this is true, then we should be able to discover a correspondence between certain kinds of personalities and certain kinds of societies, and between other kinds of personalities and other kinds of societies. For example, a military, expansionist society would likely correspond to an assertive, aggressive personality. A society with an otherworldly orientation would likely correspond to a more passive, contemplative personality. We have already seen, in the case of Edgerton's work, the correspondence between a constrained and resentful personality among sedentary farmers, on the one hand, and, on the other hand, an exuberant, expressive personality among nomadic pastoralists.

How does this happy correspondence between personality and society, so convenient for anthropologists, come about? The mediating process is child socialization. Parents have some idea what the main values and ideals of their society are, how these values and ideals define success, and what the proper procedures are for gaining success. One is more likely to fit in, and to do well, if one is a certain kind of person, the kind of person reflecting societal values, and the kind of person for whom the processes to gain success are congenial. For example, in a bellicose society, boys would be trained by their parents, who would want their boys to succeed, to be tough, to be ready to fight, to take punishment without flinching, to develop fighting skills, and so on. Here is the model as set out by LeVine (1966:18):

> Our theory involves the following causal chain:
>
> status mobility system → parental values (that is, a concept of the ideal successful man) → child-rearing practices → personality frequencies (for example percentage of population members high in n Achievement or obedience-compliance dispositions).

So in different cultural settings, people, on average, will have different personality dispositions in conformity with the different demands of the settings. As LeVine (1966:18) puts it, "A status mobility system, by favoring one set of personal qualities over another, will affect the frequency of relevant personality traits in the population."

The particular personality characteristic that LeVine is investigating is called "n Achievement," meaning "need [for] achievement." This is an established psychological concept that had been previously examined in a variety of settings, where there was usually a strong correlation between n Achievement and economic standing. LeVine (1966:12) explains n Achievement as follows:

> The term is defined as a latent disposition to compete with a standard of excellence, and involves both a persistent desire for such competition and an emotional concern with it. . . . The motive is expressed by the individual as affective concern about, or preoccupation with: doing well in relation to achievement goals, unique accomplishment, long-term commitment to the attainment of such goals, instrumental acts directed toward their attainment, obstacles to be overcome, and prospects of success or failure.

LeVine's research is directed at discovering if n Achievement (hereafter: NA) varies in the three groups—the Hausa, Yoruba, and Ibo—and whether any variation found is correlated with current professional, economic, and political achievement, and whether any variation is correlated with the status mobility systems found in these three cultures.

The test groups were comparable Hausa, Ibo, and Yoruba students, all male, from the top grades of secondary grammar schools in Zaria for the Hausa, Onitsha for the Ibo, and Ibadan for the Yoruba. Each boy spoke the language of the region at home and had parents from communities in the heartland of that group. Parents' schooling was also considered. In the first test, each student was given a half hour to write in English a description of his most recent night dream, and of another dream he had had more than once. The results, viewed by the researchers, were not even assumed to be actual dreams; all that was assumed was that "they were fantasies produced in response to an ambiguous stimulus that did not dictate or bias the content of the story" (LeVine 1966:52). The test results, or protocols, were coded simply as to whether achievement imagery was present or absent. The coders did not know the hypothesis of the study, or the ethnic groups involved; thus the coding was "blind," avoiding the possibility of expectation bias in the coding. In other words, the coding was done objectively. Agreement among the coders was high, raising confidence in the assessment. Here are a couple of examples: First, a snippet from a description scored as having achievement imagery: "I dashed for the ball and after beating Ghana's right fullback, sent in a fiery shot which left Ghana's goalkeeper sprawling on the ground." Next, a snippet from one without achievement imagery: "I invited her into my bedroom so that I could ask what the matter was. She entered with me, sat on my laps, and I—you know— . . . by the time she left my laps my dream had become a wet one" (LeVine 1966:54, 56).

What were the results in each ethnic group? The percentage of achievement imagery dreamers in each ethnic group were as follows:

Ibo	43%
southern Yoruba (Christian)	35%
northern Yoruba (Muslim)	27%
Hausa	17%

These results are consistent with the hypothesis that status mobility systems in the traditional cultures vary, that some encourage achievement motivation and some encourage obedience-compliance, and that Ibo culture encouraged achievement the most, Yoruba next, and Hausa the least. To illustrate, let us set out some of the main features of the status mobility systems of these groups, as described by anthropologists who have lived amongst them:

The Ibo (LeVine 1966:32–37) were forest village dwellers in south-eastern Nigeria. The population of some seven million were divided amongst more than 200 independent polities, each consisting of one or more villages or dispersed settlements within a specified territory. In other words, the Ibo lived in small, autonomous polities, with no supralocal centralization. Each village polity was led by councils of elders highly responsive to public opinion. The community was organized into patrilineal descent groups, but as well had one or another of age grades, title societies, individual title systems, or secret men's societies. All of these organizations served to advance cultural ideals and to allocate differentially community recognition, status, and prestige. Simon Ottenberg (quoted by LeVine 1966:34–35) says:

> The Ibo are a highly individualistic people. While a man is dependent on his family, lineage, and residential grouping for support and backing, strong emphasis is placed on his ability to make his own way in the world. . . .

> The possibilities of enhancing status and prestige are open to virtually all individuals. . . . Ibo society is thus, in a sense, an "open" society in which positions of prestige, authority, and leadership are largely achieved.

Status could be achieved through success in farming, trading, crafts, fishing, religion, and secular political leadership. There was an emphasis among the Ibo on skill, enterprise, and initiative. Upward status mobility was a function of a man's individual achievements.

Very well studied by anthropologists, the Hausa (LeVine 1966:25–32), with a population of more than eight million, lived in autocratic kingdoms that were the result of conquest by Fulani Muslims and the further conquest and enslavement of pagan peoples of Northern Nigeria. The king, who might owe fealty to a stronger king elsewhere, had in his gift numerous political offices to which were attached fiefs from which the officeholder could collect taxes or tribute, some of which he could keep along with whatever was forwarded to the king. As LeVine (1966:26) describes it:

> Commands flowed from the top down, and disobedience could be punished by removal from office . . .; tax and tribute from fiefs and vassal chiefdoms flowed from the bottom up, with each officeholder deducting his part. In the frequent wars and slave raids, officeholders raised troops in their fiefs for the king and were handsomely rewarded with booty and captive slaves. So long as an officeholder retained the favor of the king through demonstrations of loyalty and obedience, he was allowed to overtax and keep the surplus himself as well as to exceed his formal authority in a number of other says. Thus the system had a despotic character, turning on relations of dependence and power between subordinates and their superiors.

Between rulers and slaves were Hausa freemen, whose hereditary occupations were ranked. As regards status mobility, LeVine (1966:27) explains:

> The principal means of rising socially, for those of both Fulani and Hausa ancestry, was by becoming the client or follower of someone of higher status . . . who would reward his loyal client with appointment to office if he himself was successful in obtaining an official position.

Achieving political office was a means of achieving economic success, for the office enabled the holder to extract wealth from subjects. Slaves were one of the main sources of labor and were thus themselves a major economic asset. However, patrons who fell out of favor and lost position, took their clients down with them. This system of status mobility, primarily a framework of patrons and clients, demanded loyalty and obedience to those in authority. Subservience and compliance were characteristics demanded of clients. Individual autonomy, individual initiative, and self-reliant action were discouraged by this system.

Comparing status mobility systems among the Ibo and Hausa, the differences stand out clearly. Among the Ibo, success was by individual achievement, and economic success led to political standing. Among the Hausa, success through clientage to a higher-status individual and political office led to economic rewards. The qualities appreciated by the Hausa were subservience, obedience, and loyalty, while the qualities appreciated by the Ibo were self-reliance, initiative, individual abilities, and energy. "By Ibo standards, the Hausa ideal was overdependent and confining to the individual; by Hausa standards, the Ibo ideal was dangerously selfish and anarchic" (LeVine 1966:37). The Ibo system was more congenial to a man with NA, the Hausa less so. It would be expected therefore that NA would be found in greater frequency among the Ibo than among the Hausa.

Also well-known from anthropological research were the Yoruba, who honored an ancient tradition of kingship. The king, in the multiple Yoruba kingdoms, was however primarily a ritual figure, with political power residing in the hands of councils of state manned by hereditary chiefs, leaders of towns and associational, often occupational, groups, and territorial leaders. Power being distributed among the various self-governing groups in Yoruba society, there was little centralization. Political office among the Yoruba did not come with fiefs, and so economic wealth did not follow office. Beyond the internal structure of Yoruba society, there was a great deal of military adventurism, slave raiding and slave trading. Warriors were often rewarded with land, slaves, booty, and new titles. So in the Yoruba status mobility system there were internal tracks of office, but also external tracks of entrepreneurial military campaigns; the former favoring conformity and obedience, the latter favoring initiative. In traditional status mobility systems, the Yoruba fall between the rigidly hierarchical Hausa and the entrepreneurial Ibo; thus the incidence of NA among the Yoruba would be expected to fall between that of the Ibo and the Hausa.

The second test that LeVine gave to his Nigerian students was assigned essays, each given a half hour, on the topics "What is a successful man?" and "How does a boy become a successful man?" There were many enthusiastic answers. One snippet is "Hard work and success are twin-born. None can go without the other." In fact, each student had much to say about accomplishment and excellence. So universal was the response, that the results of the evaluation for NA showed only tiny differences between the ethnic groups, not in the direction expected, but not statistically significant in any case. LeVine's NA hypothesis was not borne out by the results. Why? LeVine concluded that the assignment, as a stimulus, was not sufficiently ambiguous, did not allow the students to say what was on their minds, but rather led them in too determined a fashion to give a particular kind of answer. However, the essays were also coded for obedience-social-compliance (OSC). The criteria for OSC were "unquestioned obedience to those in positions of authority, undiscriminating emulation of respected persons, respect for authority as leading to success, and compliance to the desires of peers and subordinates" (LeVine 1966:68). It was expected that on OSC the Hausa would be highest, the Ibo lowest, and the Yoruba in between. The results (LeVine 1966:68) were:

Hausa	0.29
Yoruba	−0.09
Ibo	−0.20

The Hausa were highest in OSC, the Ibo lowest, and the Yoruba in between, as expected. Furthermore, the results of OSC are the converse of NA found in the dream essays; that is, among the groups in which NA is high, OSC is low, and where NA is low, OSC is high.

LeVine also reports findings from the research of others. For example, he cites the results of a nationwide public opinion survey of social attitudes in Nigeria, done the same year as his own study. One open-ended question asked about hopes and dreams, and the respondents' best possible future. The percentage of those from different ethnic groups mentioning self-improvement as a leading aspiration varied in a pattern consistent with LeVine's NA results:

Ibo	25%
Yoruba	22%
Hausa	10%

So too with a question about hopes and dreams for the future of Nigeria, in which answers that mentioned improved standards of living through technological advance varied according to ethnic group:

Ibo	56%
Yoruba	49%
Hausa	26%

These findings are consistent with professional achievement in Nigerian society, where the early and strong performance of Yoruba has been rapidly matched by Ibo. For example, in the early 1920s, there were 12 Nigerian doctors: eight Yoruba and four native foreigners. Thirty years later, in the early 1950s, there were 160 Nigerian physicians: 76 Yoruba, 49 Ibo, and one Hausa, plus 34 others. In 30 years, the Ibo went from no doctors at all to 30 percent of all Nigerian doctors. Similar results can be found in other professions, in intellectual life, in the arts, and in politics and government.

The correspondence among the various findings presented by LeVine indicates that a clear pattern in ethnic differences in personality, particularly in motivation, has emerged. These differences also correspond with the status mobility systems of the traditional cultures of the Hausa, Yoruba, and Ibo. The response of the different ethnic groups to changing conditions and new opportunities in Nigeria—resulting from the British imperial occupation and then Nigerian independence—reflected the personality orientations rooted in the traditional status mobility systems of each ethnic group. The remarkable, historical "awakening" of the Ibo and the stolid resistance of the Hausa were driven by the different orientations of the members of these groups, orientations to such personality factors as independence, initiative, and achievement for the Ibo, and authority, compliance, and deference for the Hausa.

Chapter Six

Survey Comparisons

Anthropologists commonly pursue their research through "participant observation," living amongst the people of a particular group or locality or activity, getting to know them through face-to-face observation and exchange. So anthropologists get to know a village, or a town quarter, or a herding camp, or an occupational group pretty well. But there is always a nagging question about the extent to which that village or camp is like the other villages or camps, that is, whether the few people known are representative of the many people in that society and culture. For example, are the Kurdish villages that Fredrik Barth reported on representative of Iraqi Kurdistan generally? That is, if he had done his research in other villages, would he have had the same findings? As well, there is also the parallel question of whether conclusions drawn about that culture or society are applicable more widely, to other cultures and societies. Would David Riches' "holistic person" found among Inuit and English New Agers turn up in other cultures also striving to implement equality?

Is there any way to solve the problem of representativeness? One solution is a survey comparison, in which all cases, e.g., all villages, all camps, or all cultures, or a representative sample of all cases, would be surveyed. Such comprehensive research would insure that findings do apply to the larger society studied, or to society in general. This kind of survey approach is not very compatible with the ethnographer's conventional research methodology of participant observation, due to the vast increase of effort and time that would be required. However, stepping back from the firsthand field research of the ethnographer, taking up the role of the social anthropologist or sociologist, the researcher could draw on the research reports of others, thus using secondary sources, for broader surveys. This is exactly what George Peter Murdock did in his ground-breaking work, *Social Structure* (1949), based on reports from 250 societies around the world.

FAMILY AND KINSHIP

This topic has become a matter of concern in the United States and Canada for the past couple of decades, and continues to be important in the second decade of the 21st century. Public and official discussions involve diverse questions, including whether minority polygamous sects of Mormons engage in abuse of minors through forced or underage marriages, whether legalized homosexual marriage would open the door to legalized polygamous marriages, and whether Muslim immigrants are engaged in stealth polygyny by claiming wives as sisters, cousins, or nieces. In all of these cases, the starting point of the discussion is the well-established North American legal and moral norm of monogamy. As with all such norms, there is a strong sense that it represents the reasonable and decent way of ordering life. Some people feel that it is the "natural" way, pointing to various species of animals that pair for life.

However, as in most all cultural matters, people do things differently in different places. We can ask how normal monogamy is among cultures around the world. Murdock (1949:24), based on his survey comparison, has an answer. Of the 250 societies he studied, only 43 had strict monogamy, whereas 195 allowed polygamy (including polygyny, marriage with two or more wives, and polyandry, marriage with two or more husbands), the remaining 12 presumably lacked the relevant information. Among peoples and cultures of the world, the statistical norm, by a long way, is acceptance of polygynous marriage. Of course, cultural acceptance does not indicate a behavioral norm; the majority in a society might still have monogamous marriages, often because men cannot afford more than one wife. (North Americans are allowed to own airplanes, yachts, and tropical islands, but not many do.) Nonetheless, the acceptance of polygyny is the runaway statistical norm for world societies.

Polygyny should not be confused with the extension of sexual rights to in-laws, a widespread practice present even in monogamous unions. In this practice, married women may have sexual relations with her brothers-in-law, or, in more restricted cases, only junior brothers-in-law, while a married man may have sexual congress with his sisters-in-law. In Murdock's (1949:25) calculation, of those societies about which there is information on this topic, 41, or considerably more than half, have instituted such privileges. Such customs derive from the treatment of the members of a sibling group as a unity, sometimes called identity of the sibling group. With sibling unity in mind, the well-known customs of levirate and sororate will not come as a surprise. Levirate is the rule that a widow will marry the brother of her deceased husband; in the sororate, a widower marries the sister of his deceased wife. Murdock (1949:29) finds that, although there is no information on 65 societies, of those for which we have information, levirate and sororate are normatively preferential in 127, whereas they are not normatively preferential, and happen only rarely, in 58. Restriction to levirate with junior brothers is found in 28 societies, while restriction to junior sisters is found in nine societies. In polygynous societies, a man sometimes marries sisters contemporaneously, a practice called sororal polygyny; in polyandrous societies, a women may contemporaneously marry brothers, a practice called fraternal polyandry. So while monogamy might seem "natural" and moral to us, we are definitely in the minority among world cultures. In fact, in contemporary North American society, with many people living in "common law" marriages, that is, without marrying, and around half of all formal marriages ending in divorce, our current practice might be better described as "serial polygamy," as we move from one union to another and then to another.

When marriage takes place, it is usually more than just an agreement between the marrying couple. In the great majority of cases reviewed by Mudock—163 cases out of 241—some kind of payment is made to the family of the bride: bride-price, exchange of women between families or groups, or bride-service in which the groom works for his wife's family for an appreciable period. This is particularly marked when there is a residence rule of patrilocality, in which the bride goes to live with her husband's family. This gives us a hint of what is behind this practice: the loss of the bride to her family and community. Murdock (1949:21) confirms this by looking at how often the bride is removed from her local community, and its relation with some kind of marriage payment:

Bride usually or always leaves: 56 societies require payment; 4 do not
Bride sometimes or often leaves: 33 societies require payment; 8 do not
Bride rarely or never leaves: 6 societies require payment; 6 do not

Certainly the loss of the bride to the community is correlated with required payment. Murdock (1949:21) mentions some exceptional cases that actually prove the rule:

> Among the Abelam, for example, the usual bride-price is omitted when the married couple come from the same hamlet. Among the Copper Eskimo, if a daughter remains in the community after marriage, she and her husband render assistance to her parents and no bride-price is required, but in the exceptional case of a patrilocal intervillage marriage the groom must compensate his bride's parents for the loss.

In Indonesia there is a practice called *ambil-anak*, in which the normal patrilocal rule is waived when a family has only daughters, so that at least one son-in-law will come to live with them and take the role of a son. In this case, the usual bride-price is not paid.

As we have seen, the residence rule is important in people's lives and is thus tied to other customs and practices, such as bridewealth. The distribution of residence rules among societies is not even; patrilocality dominates: out of 250 cases, the incidence of each type is as follows:

Patrilocal	146
Matrilocal	38
Matri-patrilocal	22
Bilocal (either)	19
Neolocal (new)	17
Avunculocal	8

"Matri-patrilocal" involves initial years residing with the bride's family, followed by permanent residence with the groom's. I (Salzman 2000) am familiar with this practice from observing it among the Baluch. For some purposes, it could fairly be classed with patrilocal residence. With such an adjustment, the patrilocal category would include 168 cases, or 67 percent of all cases. We shall see a bit later why this finding is important.

With an established household, what kinds of work do people do? Is the traditional Western stereotype of women working in the home and men going out "to make a living" confirmed by ethnographic evidence? Murdock (1949:213) found that

> the tasks assigned to women in more than 75 per cent of the societies with relevant information are grain grinding, water carrying, cooking, the gathering of fuel and vegetable products, the manufacture and repair of clothing, the preservation of meat and fish, pottery making, weaving, and the manufacture of mats and baskets. . . . Most of these tasks can be carried on in the house or its immediate vicinity, and . . . none of them requires an intimate knowledge of the tribal terrain.

The picture is quite different in regard to men's work:

> The tasks assigned to men in more than 75 per cent of the sample societies, however, include the following: herding (84%), fishing (86%), lumbering (92%), trapping (95%), mining and quarrying (95%), hunting (98%), and the catching of sea mammals (99%). All of these activities, as well as the characteristic masculine pursuit of war, carry the men far from the dwelling and demand a thorough knowledge of the environs of the community and the locale of all its usable resources.

Thus, in the societies Murdock studied, men moved throughout their home territory, much more than women did, to do their work. For men, familiarity with the territory is a huge asset in pursuing a living. Knowing where to hunt, where to fish, where there are good defensive points, and so on, could mean the difference between doing well or doing badly, or worse. Murdock suggests that the benefit of working in a territory that you know goes a long way in accounting for the dominance of patrilocality as a residence pattern. Brides go to live with their new husbands because it is a benefit to the family for the husband to know his territory well. Furthermore, as some productive activities take cooperation, a man will already have cooperative experience with his kinsmen, and this also contributes to productivity in the known territory.

Marriage is one of the main ways in which sex is regulated so as to avoid disruptive sexual competition in the other cooperative relationships upon which social life depends. But it is usually accompanied by complementary norms and rules that restrict sex. North American society has traditionally limited legitimate sex to marriage partners, and at the time that Murdock was writing, this norm was largely in force. It is one of only three societies in the sample of 118 (on which information was available) that has (or had) a generalized taboo on extramarital sex. The other 115 societies had more permissive regulations:

- 49 had permissive premarital sex relations
- 3 had fully or conditionally permitted adultery
- 23 had sexually privileged relationships
- 40 had two or all three of the above

In many societies, particular relationships were identified as legitimate for extramarital relations. These were usually defined by spousal relations:

- 34 societies out of 56 (having the relevant information) freely or conditionally permitted sex relations with brother's wife
- 28 of 43 freely or conditionally permitted sex relations with wife's sister

The permitted parties were those deemed, among the population in general, closest to a spouse, and therefore legitimately subject to an extension of sexual access.

Premarital sexual access also follows the same rationale. Kin relations who are marriage partners are often deemed legitimate premarital sex partners, while kin relations who are forbidden as marriage partners are usually forbidden as premarital sexual partners. If we take the case of cross cousins, i.e., father's sister's daughter and mother's brother's daughter, we find the following regulations:

- Where cross cousin marriage is allowed, premarital relations with cross cousins are allowed in 24 societies, while forbidden in 5.

- Where cross cousin marriage is forbidden, premarital relations with cross cousins are allowed in 0 societies, and are forbidden in 72.

So while the range of legitimate sex relations is broader in most societies than a ban on extramarital relations, extramarital sex relations tend to be defined, and legitimated, with reference to marriage relations.

HUNTERS AND GATHERERS

Murdock's view of the dominance of patrilocality due to the benefits of men staying in their home territory to make a living was widespread among anthropologists in the mid-20th century. Considering hunting and gathering bands, for example, Julian H. Steward, in *Theory of Culture Change*, put forward the model of "the patrilineal band." Steward (1955:122) specifies that the patrilineal band

> is a cultural type whose essential features—patrilineality, patrilocality, exogamy, land ownership, and lineage composition—constituted a cultural core which recurred cross-culturally with great regularity.

But with the reporting of ethnographic research on hunters and gatherers in the mid-1960s, ten years after Steward's findings, a new view rapidly gained popularity. Richard Lee and Irven DeVore in *Man the Hunter* (1968) gave the first reports on Lee's work with the !Kung (now called the Ju'/hoansi, pronounced Ju-twasi) in the Kalahari Desert of southern Africa. The !Kung, according to Lee's ground-breaking research:

- spent only some four hours a day on making a living, and otherwise had a great deal of leisure,
- relied on women's gathering for the majority of their calories,
- were highly egalitarian,
- were bilateral rather than patrilineal,
- were bilocal or neolocal rather than patrilocal,
- had pervious group boundaries allowing peoples to move from band to band easily, and
- were peaceful rather than warlike.

These findings were highly congenial to North American anthropologists during a period when many were opposing the ongoing Vietnam war, when many thought the "counter-culture" rebellion against "bourgeois society" was on the right track, and when many were actively supporting the early surge of the Women's Movement (later: Feminist Movement). Lee's model of hunters and gatherers based on the !Kung provided an example of a peaceful society that many anthropologists thought we should emulate in our own society. So too with !Kung equality, seen as an appealing example to follow by supporters of the "counter-culture" rebellion. Lee also showed the predominant importance of women in providing food for the !Kung, which provided an attractive example of the importance of women for supporters of the Women's Movement.

For many, the !Kung came to be thought of as paradigmatic hunters and gatherers (recently called "foragers" by some, to avoid the hunting/gathering distinction). But are the !Kung really representative of hunters and gatherers in general? This is the question taken up by Carol. R. Ember in "Myths about Hunter-Gatherers" (1978). She examined, using the *Ethnographic Atlas* (Murdock 1967), the questions of hunter-gatherer residence patterns, subsistence activities, and conflict.

Examining residence among hunter-gatherers, Ember (1978: Table 1) found that, among 179 cases:

- 62% are patrilocal
- 29% are matrilocal
- 16% are bilocal
- 3% are avunculocal
- 2% are neolocal

So in spite of whatever preferences we may have for bilocality or neolocality as distinct from patrilocality, which for some implied dominance of men, Ember's survey comparison indicates that patrilocality among hunter-gatherers is predominant.

As regards the relative importance of gathering vs. hunting, Ember (1978:Table 2) found:

- 10% of cases show gathering contributes more than half the calories
- 13% show that gathering contributes around half the calories
- 77% show that gathering contributes less than half the calories

On the question of who contributes more foodstuffs, Ember (1978: Table 4) found that

- 8% of cases are of women contributing more than men
- 9% of cases are women contributing about the same amount as men
- 83% of cases are in which men contribute more than women

So the !Kung model of hunters and gatherers, in which women gathering provides the majority of calories, is highly exceptional among hunters and gatherers in general. Ember shows that men hunting are the main contributors of subsistence for hunting and gathering groups worldwide.

A review of the frequency of warfare among hunters and gatherers speaks to the question of how peaceful hunters and gatherers are. Ember (1978:Table 5) found that

- 20 (65%) hunting and gathering peoples engaged in warfare more than once every two years.
- 8 (26%) hunting and gathering peoples engaged in warfare less frequently than once every two years
- 3 (10%) hunting and gathering peoples, including the !Kung, engaged in warfare only rarely.

So the !Kung model of hunters and gatherers as idyllic, peaceful peoples is not substantiated by Ember's survey comparison. Rather, some 66 percent of hunting and gathering peoples engage in warfare fairly frequently, and only 10 percent engage in warfare rarely.

It appears that hunters and gatherers are not the egalitarian, feminist, pacifist models that some anthropologists crave. Ember is able, through a survey comparison, to provide a more realistic picture of hunters and gatherers.

Chapter Seven

Conclusions

Anthropologists as students of society and culture cannot conduct experiments on people. We cannot say, switch your principle of descent from patrilineal to matrilineal, and we will watch to see what happens to your other institutions. We cannot say, stop farming and start herding cattle, and we will see whether your temperament changes. Even if we could, we wouldn't, and shouldn't. However, there are "natural experiments," similarities and differences and many varieties of society and culture already out there in the world. By observing them, we can gain some of the same insight that comes from laboratory experiments. A valuable tool in observing and understanding is, as I have tried to illustrate throughout this book, comparative analysis. But as will be clear by now, comparative analysis is not a single approach. Rather, it is a quiver with a number of arrows. We have seen that some anthropologists have used comparison primarily to elicit commonalities from a variety of settings, some have used it primarily to juxtapose contrasting cases, others have focused on comparisons of sibling cases with much in common, while yet others have made their comparisons as broad and inclusive as possible. Comparative analysis generously lends itself to a variety of anthropological purposes.

Anthropologists generally wear two hats: On the one hand, we are ethnographers, studying the contours of one or more particular societies, usually through the down on the ground, out in the field, research strategy of participant observation of a limited population. On the other hand, as social and cultural anthropologists, we try to take a broader view, encompassing a wide range of societies and cultures. To do this, we usually draw on the "ethnographic literature," that is, the reports of ethnographic research by our ethnographer colleagues. For example, Robert LeVine in *Dreams and Deeds* (1966) builds a picture of the traditional

91

cultures of the Ibo, Hausa, and Yoruba by drawing on the ethnographic reports of anthropologists who did ethnographic field research among those peoples. So anthropology, like all other academic disciplines, is a collective project, in which we build on our anthropological ancestors, draw on our contemporaries, and try to guide our descendants.

Which brings me to the question of how comparative analysis can serve your intellectual and research purposes, whether as an anthropologist, an academic in a different field, in business or government, or as an aware citizen observing the world and considering options. I would suggest that any examination of aspects of society and culture would benefit from comparisons with other cases, to contextualize any particular case examined, to highlight features of the case examined, to indicate likely connections between features of interest and other features present, and to pursue and challenge any general understandings. Comparison can assist us in disciplining our thoughts and thus support sounder understanding. To illustrate further, let us consider a topic of current interest, social and cultural change and development, and the way in which one might use comparison to advantage.

Neither society nor culture is static. Even when they are maintaining the same form, reproduction of customs and institutions is ongoing and dynamic. But there are also many processes, some of them cumulative, that lead to structural change. How change comes about, and its consequences, are unavoidably topics of great interest to students of culture and society.

One kind of comparison that we have seen in Hackenburg's account of the Pima and Papago is comparison between different time periods in the life of a particular society, in order to understand what changed and the factors that led to change. Another example is Pauline Kolenda's analysis in *Caste in Contemporary India* (1985[1978]), comparing traditional caste practice with contemporary dynamics, thus showing the transformation in modern times of caste as an institution and set of practices. A more specific and more detailed study is Donald Attwood's *Raising Cane: The Political Economy of Sugar in Western India* (1992), which offers several kinds of comparison: an historical one showing the development of irrigated sugar cultivation and of cooperative sugar factories, a geographical comparison between irrigated and nonirrigated regions, and an institutional comparison between cooperative, private, and government sugar factories. Broader, regionally and institutionally, is the comparison among cooperatives of various types in different regions of India, set out in *Finding the Middle Path: The Political Economy of Cooperation in Rural India* (1995), B. S. Baviskar and Donald W. Attwood, editors.

Laurel Bossen in *The Redivision of Labor: Women and Economic Choice in Four Guademalan Communities* (1984) offers three main comparisons: an historical comparison of the earlier subsistence economy with the later commercial economy; a comparison of four social segments: the Maya peasantry, the plantations, the urban poor, and the middle class; and a gender comparison between women and men. Among her many findings, she discovers that women, who had a major role in production and control in the subsistence economy, have become sidelined in the commercial economy, losing status and control, showing that everyone does not benefit equally from modernization. Hernando de Soto—not an anthropologist, but a researcher to whom I would grant honorary anthropological status—in his acclaimed book, *The Mystery of Capital: Why Capitalism Triumphs in the West and Fails Everywhere Else* (2000), compares the West, where the legal system is secure and efficient, and private property is widespread, with the rest, where the legal system is weak and inefficient, and legal private property is rare. De Soto's point is that legal private property is value that can provide capital, and that the untold billions of dollars of nonlegalized property could, if legalized, enrich the poor of the underdeveloped countries.

For future studies in international development, one strategy would be to compare countries and regions that have been successful in development, where there is a high level of production and a high standard of living, health, and human welfare, with countries or regions where, in contrast, the level of production is relatively low, as is standard of living, health, and human welfare. De Soto's research is one effort to identify the critical causal factors through such a comparison. Regions within countries also differ in degree of development. Two regions in which I have carried out research, Baluchistan in Iran and Sardinia in Italy, were poorer and less developed in comparison to other regions in those countries. So too with larger, multinational regions, such as the Arab countries, which are moderately developed, and East Asian nations, which are highly developed (*Arab Human Development Report* 2002).

To enrich studies of development, a comparison over time, from one period to the next in societies or regions, could be added. Societies at more or less the same level at one point in time are in some instances at a later point in time at quite different levels, one having remained fairly static, or fallen behind, the other having advanced considerably. For example, to take one of many possible criteria in assessing development, in 1981, China was producing half the output of scientific papers of the Arab world; by 1987, its output had equaled that of Arab countries; by 2000, it produced double their output. By this criterion, and by most others, China was developing at a much faster pace than Arab countries (*Arab Human Development Report* 2002:66).

There has been a strong trend almost everywhere in the world toward urbanization. As urban industry and commerce have developed, and rural agriculture become more efficient and productive, and less labor-intensive, people have flowed out of the countryside and into cities. Anthropologists would like to understand how peoples' ideas and relationships continue and are transformed by the rural-urban transition. For example, when Indians leave their villages and migrate to cities, what changes for them? What happens to their caste membership? How do they relate to people in the new setting? Pauline Kolenda in *Caste in Contemporary India* (1985[1978]) gives us some suggestive leads to follow up: Caste groups that are traditionally identified with particular occupational categories often adopt a new, industrial occupational affinity. While still ordering marriage through caste endogamy, the caste group becomes an interest group.

> In relation to the political, economic, and educational institutions of the modern secular sector of Indian society, the kin-community functions primarily as a supplier of competent personnel. The descent group serves as a resource network for kin-community members seeking access to the modern occupational structure. While such a network of "brothers" usually functions largely on an informal basis, some kin-communities do have voluntary organizations or even political parties associated with them. Such organizations are typically composed of modern-sector participants who try to advance the welfare of the kin-community through contacts and exchanges with schools and universities and the government at various levels. The kin-community and its associated interest groups compete with other interest groups for political power, job training, and job placement. (Kolenda 1985[1978]:147–148)

One possible comparison, arising from the hierarchical nature of the caste system, would be between higher and lower castes as they adapt to urban conditions. Another would be between first-generation migrants and second- and third-generation migrants, in relation to caste and other aspects of their lives. Some of this research is ongoing, but there is much more to learn, especially as India develops at a torrid pace.

In Africa, too, urbanization proceeds apace. There, of course, the rural background is not caste, but tribe. (Some anthropologists now think that we shouldn't call these groups "tribes," but Africans still do so.) What role do tribes play in urban Africa? A comparison between rural and urban tribesmen would clarify this question. Another potentially illuminating comparison, suggested by Edgerton's *Individual in Cultural Adaptation* (1971), would be between Africans with agricultural backgrounds and those with pastoral backgrounds in their urban adaptations. Would the differing rural occupational and temperamental backgrounds influence urban occupations, relations, and success? Such correspondences are also suggested by LeVine in *Dreams and Deeds* (1966), in which we have learned that differences in ethnic status mobility systems in traditional Nigeria led to differences in performance in modern, urban Nigeria. An African interregional comparison could be made between East Africa, where cities were not well developed in precolonial times, and West Africa, where cities were well established in precolonial times, to see if there are differences in the ways cities have developed, and whether they have maintained different patterns or have increasingly converged.

Anthropologists are not interested only in major cultural contrasts and parallels, and in exotic overseas cultures and societies, but wish to understand people in all social and cultural settings. Medical anthropologists study AIDs, drug use, and even fetal monitors, and cultural anthropologists study topics such as drug gangs, prisons, abortion, and retirement communities. Here too comparative analysis is a valuable tool. The significance of fetal monitors in birth processes can most illuminatingly be studied in comparison with birth processes absent fetal monitors. A study of abortion might usefully include a comparison between teenage women who had abortions and those who did not and carried to term. A time comparison, a decade later, of the same women, as to their own assessment of their decision, their occupational and economic status, and their family and social relations, could be instructive.

For anthropologists, and others as well, there are almost an infinite number of attractive places to go and topics to research. In most research, comparative analysis provides perspective and aids insight. Why even try to do research without it?

Bibliography

Aguirre, B. E. 2000. "Social Control in Cuba," unpublished paper. A later version was published in *Latin American Politics and Society* 44(2):67–98.

Arab Human Development Report. 2002. New York: United Nations Development Programme. Available online: http://www.arab-hdr.org/publications/other/ahdr2002e.pdf

Assmuth, Laura. 1997. *Women's Work, Women's Worth: Changing Lifecourses in Highland Sardinia*. Transactions No. 39. Helsinki: Finnish Anthropological Society.

Attwood, Donald W. 1992. *Raising Cane: The Political Economy of Sugar in Western India*. Boulder: Westview Press.

Babeuf, Francois-Noel and Sylvain Marechal. 1997[circa 1790]. "The Manifesto of Equality," in *Equality: Selected Readings*, edited by L. P. Pojman and R. Westmoreland. New York: Oxford University Press.

Barth, Fredrik. 1953. *Principles of Social Organization in Southern Kurdistan*. Universitetets Ethnografiske Museum Bulletin No. 7. Oslo: Brødrene Jørgensen A/S.

Barth, Fredrik. 1970[1954]. "Father's Brother's Daughter Marriage in Kurdistan," in *Peoples and Cultures of the Middle East,* vol. I, edited by Louise Sweet. Garden City: The Natural History Press. (Originally published in *Southwestern Journal of Anthropology* 10:164–171.)

Baviskar, B. S. and Donald W. Attwood, eds. 1995. Finding the Middle Path: The Political Economy of Cooperation in Rural India. Boulder: Westview Press.

Benedict, Ruth. 1935[1934]. *Patterns of Culture*. London: Routledge and Kegan Paul.

Berlin, Isaiah. 1969. "Two Concepts of Liberty," in *Four Essays on Liberty*, by Isaiah Berlin. London: Oxford University Press.

Berlin, Isaiah. 1978. "The Hedgehog and the Fox," in *Russian Thinkers*, by Isaiah Berlin. London: Hogarth Press.

Bertrand, Penelope. 2009. *Living in Shadows: The Omnipresence of Illegality in Cuba's Popular Culture*. Honours Thesis. Montreal: Department of Anthropology, McGill University.

Blackwell, Tom. 2009. "Prognosis for Profit," *National Post,* 27 June, A1, A8.
Blok, Anton. 1988[1974]. *The Mafia of a Sicilian Village, 1860–1960.* Long Grove, IL: Waveland Press.
Bossen, Laurel Herbenar. 1984. *The Redivision of Labor: Women and Economic Choice in Four Guatemalan Communities.* Albany: State University of New York Press.
Caltagirone, Benedetto. 1989. *Animali perduti: Abigeato e scambio sociale in Barbagia.* Cagliari: Celt editrice.
Canada, Government of, Department of Finance. 2009. "Equalization Program," http://www.fin.gc.ca/fedprov/eqp-eng.asp
Chatty, Dawn. 1996. *Mobile Pastoralists: Development Planning and Social Change in Oman.* New York: Columbia University Press.
Cole, Donald Powell. 1975. *Nomads of the Nomads: The Al Murrah Bedouin of the Empty Quarter.* Chicago: Aldine.
Colson, Elizabeth. 1962. *The Plateau Tonga of Northern Rhodesia.* Manchester: Manchester University Press.
Carneiro, Robert L. 1961. "Slash-and-Burn Cultivation among the Kuikuru and Its Implications for Cultural Development in the Amazon Basin," *Anthropologica* Supplement 2, reprinted in *Man in Adaptation: The Cultural Present,* edited by Yehudi A. Cohen. Chicago: Aldine, 1968, 131–145.
De Gioannis, Paola, and Giuseppe Serri, eds. 1991. *La Sardegna. Cultura E Società.* Firenze: La Nuova Italia.
de Soto, Hernando. 2000. *The Mystery of Capital: Why Capitalism Triumphs in the West and Fails Everywhere Else.* New York: Basic Books.
Dyson-Hudson, Neville. 1966. *Karimojong Politics.* Oxford: Clarendon Press.
Edelsward, Lisa Marlene. 1988. "Communities of Conflict and Cooperation." Working Paper of the Mediterranean Anthropological Research Equipe. Montreal: Department of Anthropology, McGill University.
Edelsward, Lisa Marlene. 1995. *Highland Visions: Recreating Rural Sardinia.* Unpublished Ph.D. dissertation. Montreal: McGill University.
Edgerton, Robert B. 1971. *The Individual in Cultural Adaptation: A Study of Four East African Peoples.* Berkeley: University of California Press.
Ember, Carol R. 1978. "Myths about Hunter-Gatherers," *Ethnology* 17(4):439–448.
Evans-Pritchard, E. E. 1940. *The Nuer: A Description of the Modes of Livelihood and Political Institutions of a Nilotic People.* Oxford: Clarendon Press.
Evans-Pritchard, E. E. 1949. *The Sanusi of Cyrenaica.* Oxford: Clarendon Press.
Evans-Pritchard, E. E. 1951. *Kinship and Marriage among the Nuer.* Oxford: Clarendon Press.
Fabietti, Ugo, and P. C. Salzman, eds. 1996. *The Anthropology of Tribal and Peasant Pastoral Societies.* Pavia, Italy: Collegio Ghislieri; and Como, Italy: Ibis.
Fishkin, James S. 1978. "Liberty vs. Equal Opportunity," *Social Philosophy and Policy* 5(1):32–48. Reprinted in *Equality: Selected Readings,* edited by Louis P. Pojman and Robert Westmoreland. New York: Oxford University Press, 1997.
Geertz, Clifford. 1968. *Islam Observed: Religious Development in Morocco and Indonesia.* New Haven: Yale University Press.
Geertz, Clifford. 1973. *The Interpretation of Cultures.* New York: Basic Books.

Gellner, Ernst. 1969. *Saints of the Atlas*. Chicago: University of Chicago Press.

Gillespie, Kerry. 2007. "John Tory Puts Faith in School Religion," *The Toronto Star,* June 24. http://www.thestar.com/News/Ontario/article/239077

Gluckman, Max. 1959. *Custom and Conflict in Africa*. Glencoe, IL: The Free Press.

Hackenberg, Robert A. 1962. "Economic Alternatives in Arid Lands: A Case Study of the Pima and Papago Indians," *Ethnology* 2:186–196.

Hayek (von Hayek), Friedrich A. 1960. *The Constitution of Liberty*. Chicago: University of Chicago Press.

Hodgson, Dorothy L., ed. 2000. *Rethinking Pastoralism in Africa: Gender, Culture and the Myth of the Patriarchal Pastoralist*. Oxford: James Currey.

Irons, William. 1975. *The Yomut Turkmen*. Anthropology Paper No. 58. Ann Arbor: Museum of Anthropology, University of Michigan.

Johnston, David, ed. 2000. *Equality*. Indianapolis: Hackett.

Kennedy, Janice. 2009. "Symbols and Celebration," *Ottawa Citizen,* 28 June, A11.

Kolenda, Pauline. 1985[1978]. *Caste in Contemporary India*. Long Grove, IL: Waveland Press.

Lancaster, William. 1997[1981]. *The Rwala Bedouin Today* (2nd Edition). Long Grove, IL: Waveland Press.

Lee, Richard B. and Irven DeVore, eds. 1968. *Man the Hunter*. Chicago: University of Chicago Press.

Levant, Ezra. 2007. "Censorship in the Name of 'Human Rights,'" *National Post,* 18 December, A16.

Levant, Ezra. 2008. "'Human Rights' vs. Magna Carta," *National Post,* 15 January, A13.

Levant, Ezra. 2009. *Shake Down: How Our Government Is Undermining Democracy in the Name of Human Rights*. Toronto: McClelland & Stewart.

LeVine, Robert A. 1966. *Dreams and Deeds: Achievement Motivation in Nigeria*. Chicago: University of Chicago Press.

Levellers, The. 2000. [1648] "An Agreement of the People," in *Equality*, edited by David Johnston. Indianapolis: Hackett.

Lévi-Strauss, Claude. 1966. *The Savage Mind*. Translated by John Weightman and Doreen Weightman. Chicago: University of Chicago Press.

Lewis, I. M. 1961. *A Pastoral Democracy: A Study of Pastoralism and Politics among the Northern Somali of the Horn of Africa*. London: Oxford University Press.

Lewis, I. M. 1976. *Social Anthropology in Perspective*. Cambridge: Cambridge University Press.

Lindholm, Charles. 1982. *Generosity and Jealousy: The Swat Pakhtun of Northern Pakistan*. New York: Columbia University Press.

Lindholm, Charles. 2002. *The Islamic Middle East: Tradition and Change*. Malden, MA: Blackwell.

Liori, Antonangelo. 1991. *Manuale di sopravvivenza in Barbagia*. Cagliari: Edizioni della Torre.

Liori, Antonangelo. 1995. "Complicità invidia e vergogna," L'Unione Sarda, 15 maggio, p. 1.

Malinowski, Bronislaw. 1978[1935]. *Coral Gardens and Their Magic*. Mineola, New York: Dover.

Malinowski, Bronislaw. 1984[1922]. *Argonauts of the Western Pacific*. Long Grove, IL: Waveland Press.

Malinowski, Bronislaw. 1987[1929]. *The Sexual Life of Savages*. Boston: Beacon Press.

Malinowski, Bronislaw. 2009[1926]. *Crime and Custom in Savage Society*. London: Routledge and Kegan Paul.

Mill, John Stuart. 1947[1859]. *On Liberty*. Northbrook, IL: AHM.

Murdock, George Peter. 1949. *Social Structure*. New York: Macmillan.

Murdock, George Peter. 1967. "Ethnographic Atlas: A Summary," *Ethnology* 6:109–236.

Murphy, Robert F. and Julian H. Steward. 1956. "Tappers and Trappers: Parallel Process in Acculturation," *Economic Development and Cultural Change* 4:335–353.

Nadel, S. F. 1952. "Witchcraft in Four African Societies: An Essay in Comparison," *American Anthropologist* 54:18–29.

Nadel, S. F. 1953. *The Foundations of Social Anthropology*. Glencoe, IL: The Free Press.

Nuova Sardegna, la. Daily newspaper. Published in Sasseri, Sardinia.

O'Neill, Terry. 2008. "Fire the Censors," *National Post*, 23 January, A12.

O'Toole, Megan. 2009. "French Education Comes Under Fire," *National Post*, 27 June, A8.

Peters, Emrys L. 1990. *The Bedouin of Cyrenaica*, edited by J. Goody and E. Marx. Cambridge: Cambridge University Press.

Peters, Pauline E. 1994. *Dividing the Commons: Politics, Policy, and Culture in Botswana*. Charlottesville: University Press of Virginia.

Pigliaru, Antonio. 1975[1959]. *Il banditismo in Sardegna: La vendetta barbaricina come ordinamento giuridico*. Milano: Guiffre Editore.

Pitt-Rivers, Julian. 1961[1954]. *The People of the Sierra*. Chicago: University of Chicago Press.

Ponce Solozábal, José Ramón. 2006. "Castro's Tactics of Control in Cuba," *Military Review* 86(4):90–100.

Pojman, L. P. and R. Westmoreland, eds. 1997. *Equality: Selected Readings*. New York: Oxford University Press.

Radcliffe-Brown, A. R. 1952. *Structure and Function in Primitive Society*. London: Cohen & West.

Radcliffe-Brown, A. R. 1958. *Method in Social Anthropology*. Chicago: University of Chicago Press.

Radcliffe-Brown, A. R. 1964[1922]. *The Andaman Islanders*. New York: The Free Press.

Ragolta, Francisco. 1983. "Vigilancia y Orden Público," *International Socialist Journal* 2:21.

Rawls, John. 1971. *A Theory of Justice*. Cambridge, MA: Harvard University Press.

Riches, David. 2000. "The Holistic Person: Or, the Ideology of Egalitarianism," *Journal of the Royal Anthropological Institute* (N.S.) 6:669–685.

Salzman, Philip Carl. 1978a. "Does Complementary Opposition Exist?" *American Anthropologist* 80(1):53–70.

Salzman, Philip Carl. 1978b. "Ideology and Change in Middle Eastern Tribal Societies," *Man* (N.S.) 13:618–637.

Salzman, Philip Carl. 1981. "Culture as Enhabilmentis," in *The Structure of Folk Models*, edited by L. Holy and M. Stuchlik. A.S.A. Monograph 20. London: Academic Press.

Salzman, Philip Carl. 1988. "Labour Formations in a Nomadic Tribe," in *Who Shares: Co-operatives and Rural Development*, edited by D. W. Attwood and B. S. Baviskar. Delhi: Oxford University Press.

Salzman, Philip Carl. 1996a. "Peasant Pastoralists" in *The Anthropology of Tribal and Peasant Pastoral Societies*, edited by Ugo Fabietti and P. C. Salzman. Pavia: Collegio Ghislieri, and Como: Ibis. Reprinted in Salzman 2004.

Salzman, Philip Carl. 1996b. "The Electronic Trojan Horse: Television in the Globalization of Paramodern Cultures," in *The Cultural Dimensions of Global Change: An Anthropological Approach*, edited by Lourdes Arizpe. Paris: UNESCO.

Salzman, Philip Carl. 1999a. *The Anthropology of Real Life: Events in Human Experience*. Long Grove, IL: Waveland Press.

Salzman, Philip Carl. 1999b. "Is Inequality Universal?" *Current Anthropology* 40(1):31–61.

Salzman, Philip Carl. 2000. *Black Tents of Baluchistan*. Washington, DC: Smithsonian Institution Press.

Salzman, Philip Carl. 2004. *Pastoralists: Equality, Hierarchy, and the State*. Boulder: Westview Press.

Salzman, Philip Carl. 2005. "The Iron Law of Politics," *Politics and the Life Sciences* 23:20–39.

Salzman, Philip Carl. 2008. *Culture and Conflict in the Middle East*. Amhurst, NY: Humanity Books.

Sheikh, Muneeza, Naseem Mithoowani, Khurrum Awan, Daniel Simard, and Ali Ahmed. 2007. "We Are Challenging Magazine's Islamophobic Bias," *Ottawa Citizen,* 21 December, A11.

Stern, Leonard. 2008. "Speech Impediments," *Ottawa Citizen,* 2 February, B6.

Steward, Julian A. 1955. *Theory of Culture Change: The Methodology of Multilinear Evolution*. Urbana: University of Illinois Press.

Steyn, Mark. 2000. "Canadian Health Care: No Tiers Left to Shed," *National Post,* 16 November, A18.

Tawney, R. H. 1952[1931]. *Equality* (4th Edition). London: Allen and Unwin.

Taylor, Peter Shawn. 2009. "Calgary's Living Wage Boondoggle," *National Post,* 25 March, FP17.

Unione Sarda, l'. Daily newspaper. Published in Cagliari, Sardinia.

von Hayek (see Hayek)

Warburton, Nigel. 2001. *Freedom: An Introduction with Readings*. London: Routledge.

Wikipedia. 2009. "Equalization Payments," http://en.wikipedia.org/wiki/Equalization_payments

Wolf, Eric. 1955. "Types of Latin American Peasantry." *American Anthropologist* 57:452–470.

Zygel, Philippe. 2009. "A Fake Cuban Cigar Is Never Just a Cigar," *National Post,* 28 March, FW3.

Index